# At The Millennium's End

## Small Figurative Artwork in the United States

# At the Millennium's End

## Small Figurative Artwork in the United States

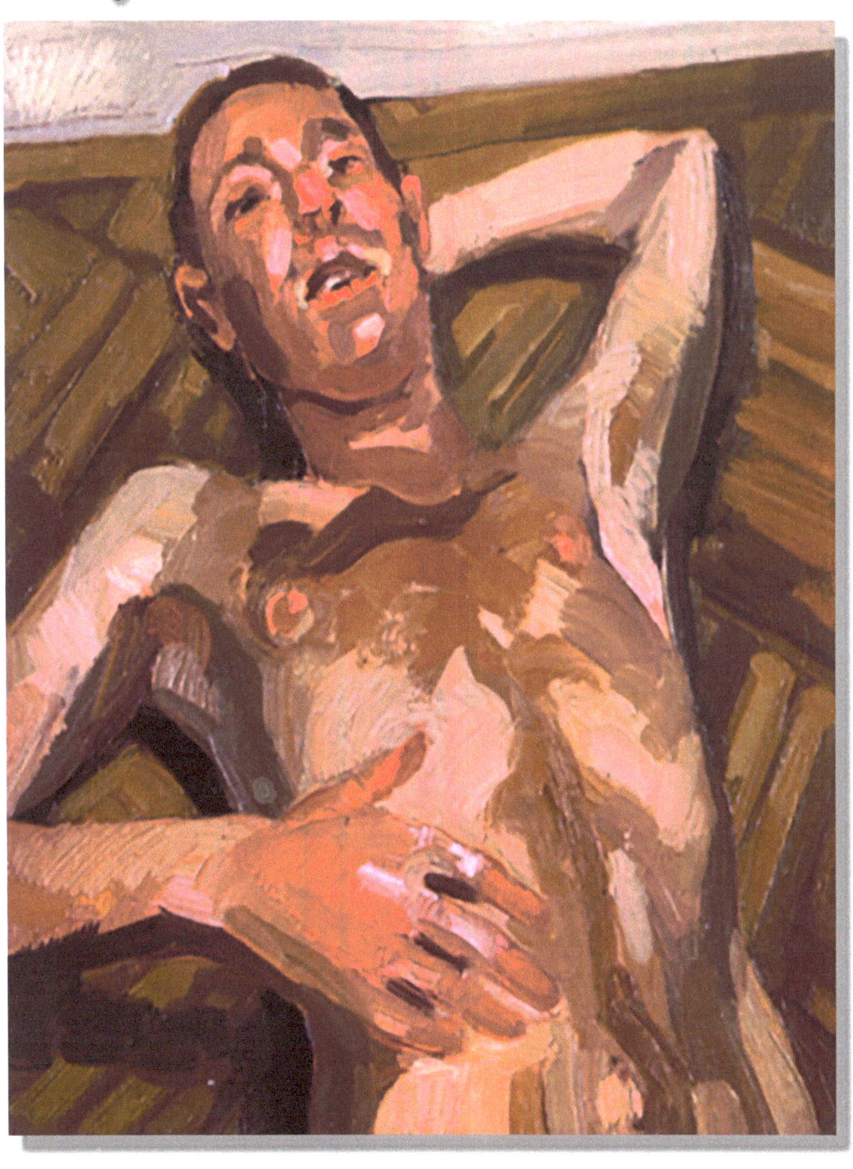

William Woolf

IFISS

COPYRIGHT

# At The Millennium's End
## Small Figurative Artwork in the United States

**William Woolf, Ph.D., M.F.A.**



Published by IFISS Press
Copyright © 1998, 2025
www.ifisspress.com
ip@ifisspress.com



paperback: ISBN-13: 978-1-937687-22-9

Artwork discussed in the book were included in a 1998 exhibition curated by William Woolf, Ph.D. titled "Current Small Figurative Work in the United States" in Tallahassee, FL.

Painting on cover: *Untitled by* Simone DiLaura

**Mysteries**

seeing shape...
touching texture

to know...
the artist stares hard

so difficult to see...
what is before you

many shapes taken...
the same, no opposite, so diverse

all... an answer
ww

# Contents

## *The Ethos and Attraction of Small Figurative Art*

The ethos of small figurative art lies in its unique ability to convey profound emotional and human experiences condensed into a compact and intimate format. This is the kind of art that links the viewer to a vast, unbroken record of human expression that stretches back 40,000 years to the earliest known figurative paintings found in the cave of Lubang Jeriji Saléh in Borneo.[1] These ancient images are a reminder that representational art is one of humanity's earliest and most enduring methods of making sense of the sensory visual world: elaborating on the figurative to tell stories, convey emotion, and share experiences.

Small representations or depictions of subjects, often populated with people, animals, or landscapes, can convey more than just a visual narrative. Figurative artworks rely on an assumed common ground of abstracted shapes, be they naturalistic, idealized, or geometric. Along with color, abstraction, metaphor, and symbolism, they produce aesthetic effects through their composition, i.e., by what is designed, which depends on factors such as line, shape, color, light, dark, mass, volume, texture, and perspective, all carefully juxtaposed.[2]

Small figurative artworks seek up-close-and-personal examination, in a way that large-scale artwork cannot. It is this intimate meeting with the viewer, inviting them to engage in a closer relationship with the art, and giving rise to an emotional response. In the small and miniature works, when the viewer looks at the art, they can see the subtle nuances in body language, facial expressions, complex narratives, and moods that are suggested, and how instinctive brushstrokes, actions, and sculptural details add up to a symbolic language; poetic expression that incites viewers to think, question, and feel.[3]

---

1 Zimmer, Carl (7 November 2018). "In Cave in Borneo Jungle, Scientists Find Oldest Figurative Painting in the World - A cave drawing in Borneo is at least 40,000 years old, raising intriguing questions about creativity in ancient societies" (https://www.nytimes.com/2018/11/07/science/oldest-cave-art-borneo.html). The New York Times. Retrieved 22 July 2025.

2 Adams, Laurie Schneider, The Methodologies of Art, Westview Press, 1996, p16-18

3 Gombrich, E. H., The Story of Art. Phaidon Press, 1967.

Art is an expressive product of the imagination.[4] It is this relationship between realism and imagination that is the common ground on which figurative art making takes place. Small figurative or depictive works of art employ many myriad subjects, such as figures (human), animals, and landscape, and can tell a lot more than just visual, story-based tales. The materials that artists use - color, abstraction, metaphor, and symbolism in an artwork - push toward the resulting narrative. In the gradation between exact representation and abstract imitation, compositions are presented that are identifiable but open to private comprehension. This dialogue confronts the audience, inviting them to look for meaning through figures that are modeled on reality but populated by poetic invention.

The size of the figurative artwork is also culturally and philosophically significant, and its scale encompasses more than mere size; it is a relative reference, frequently based on the human scale. Scale is one of the tools artists use to influence how viewers experience authority, intimacy, importance, or vulnerability. A smaller figurative piece can allow a sense of closeness or personal involvement, concentrating on emotional states that could get lost within a larger work. This kind of manipulation of scale is not just about the immediate visual sensation, but also allows general views on the place of the human being in the universe, provoking thoughts that are both personal and universal.

In these existing cultural and technological conditions, small figurative art is effective in providing viewers with a tactile, human experience unlike the frequently massive, digitally dominated scale of contemporary living. The small scale of these works, with their layers of complexity, invites mindfulness and allows for slow examination; a counterpoint to the velocity and expansiveness of digital images. Small pieces of art contribute to forming an involvement that enhances emotional resonance and reflection.

With classical inspiration, figurative art gives and receives from this tradition a living practice. Symbolism and narrative in figures turn basic photographs and drawings into intricate visual narratives rich in emotional, historical, or spiritual meaning. This can turn figurative pieces into contemplative pieces, and the viewer then stops to think and can find meaning upon meaning hidden within them in this connection of being human. The

4 Fry, Roger. "An Essay in Aesthetics." Vision and Design, London,1920, pp. 16-38

true beauty of small figurative artwork lies in this multi-leveled connection; it is intellectual, emotive, and spiritual. It allows us to discover the tension between the imaginary and the real, to experience the diversity of human expression on a smaller, human scale, and to discover our personal story in the struggles and dreams inside these miniature worlds. Such art continues to be a necessary, an eternal rejuvenating way for us to communicate; one that respects our innate desire to make sense of things through figures, and allows for ongoing reinterpretation in time, and across cultures.

# *Introduction*

These works serve as an introduction to small figurative art at the end of the last century when they were accepted into a national juried exhibition which examined the same in 1998. As such they are an excellent cross-section of the state of small figurative art in America as that century drew to a close. Visually rich, touching and intimate, these works explore small moments of identity, exposure, and human impact. These works encourage an intimate relationship between the artist and the viewer.

There are twenty-one works in this discussion and survey. Eleven are two-dimensional works and ten are three-dimensional works. Each artwork has a two page spread. On the left page for each artwork is the curator's (my) statement and the artist statement. Location is listed as known by curator at time of publishing. On the right page is an image of the artwork with title, medium, and size. *Dimensions for all pieces are in inches.*

Of the eleven two-dimensional works there are four oil paintings; three acrylic paintings; one water media; one graphite drawing; one etching; and one emulsion transfer. Bold colors predominate.

- Pat Boyer's *Legs Up I,* is a sensual water media painting on handmade paper that uses color and the recurring shape of legs raised in the air in her abstracted watercolor.

- Danny Conant's *Floating Field*, a polaroid emulsion transfer on watercolor paper, has a sensuousness in the image and technique, playing with realism of the photograph and the creativeness of the abstracting polaroid emulsion.

- Simone DiLaura's half-length torso painting, *Untitled*, stretches the male body on a parquet floor with a bold painted surface exploring a sense of male vulnerability and self-possession.

- Richard Duncan's etching, *Epitaph for a Sun Watcher*, is perhaps the most abstract figurative work in the show, with the pelvic suggestion that hints at a narrative both contemporary and ancient.

- Pieter Favier's *Amelia Series #6*, captures his wife's face with an elusive expressiveness hinting at a complex narrative, mood, and emotion through suggestion and texture rather than explicit detail.

- Jennifer Finch's *Mother and Jacob,* is a modern madonna and child based on her observations of her mother with her nephew and indicating the timelessness of certain cultural images and the intimacy of the human connection.

- Ann Holden's oil painting, *Woman at Table*, plays with an abstracted faceless figure in a space that allows for a broad range of emotional interpretations on the role of women in our culture.

- Sally Phillips' tiny and detailed graphite drawing, *The Clearing*, speaks of relationships between people, nature, and a possible symbolic relationship of the land and environment.

- Jackie (Ritke) Jones' *A Good Egg,* presents a narrative painting that requires us to look beyond the colorful folk/naive to its subtle, multi-layered meaning on the human condition, with the mixing of portraiture and psychological observation.

- Ya-Mei Su's *Secret,* directly tells the viewer something more is here, and it's up to them to figure it out while explore the interior world of the subject.

- Constance Tenhawks' *Let's Go,* has a foot tapping energy that makes one feel those red high heels on the go with joy and excitement, creating a strong emotional charisma.

Of the ten three-dimensional works in the exhibition include three bronzes, one sterling silver sculpture, two ceramic mixed-media pieces, two mixed-media, one dress and mixed-media, and one work of electroformed copper mixed-media.

- Anne Bedrick's Bronze sculpture *Perplexed,* is aptly titled; the expression on her male figure conveys this difficult to portray emotion, but one so often found in life.

- Dan Bethune's three-dimensional piece, *Independent Ego,* demonstrates that however much we may think of ourselves as independent, we all are connected to others.

- William Carmen's *Offering,* mixed-media on ceramic, is a delicate, haunting, thoughtful piece evoking a sense of mystery, introspection, and is a deeply contemplative.

- Roberto Colon's bronze sculpture *Rehbok*, one of only two works not based on the human figure, is very intimate, and discriminating with his portrayal of a mother deer and nursing fawn.

- V. Emil Dickin's bronze *Introspection I,* shows a broad back in a yoga pose that connect with emotional, historical, and spiritual indicators.

- Paige Forshay-Rodefer's construction, *It's Obvious*, is not subtle in examining the roles played by women and their thought-provoking tension between playfulness and introspection, and its implications.

- Jonnie Ihlefeld's dress, *The Unborn*, creates an ambiguity about the lives and role of women in contemporary society, using clothing as both object, metaphor, and meaning in human experience.

- Eric Marlow's tiny sterling silver figure, *Too Loose La Trek,* is elegant and minimal allowing viewers to contemplate not just what is there, but also what is intentionally left out, inviting a meditation on the essence of humanity.

- Elise Megremis' *Catwoman*, examines through subtle and not so subtle twists of humor, using animal characteristics, what society says about women, what women are taught in our culture, and subsequently, what roles they perform?

- Phillip Soosloff's playful clay, mixed-media piece, *A Tough Nut To Crack*, reflects the delicate nature of emotional recovery and self-exploration, capturing the dynamics of the therapist-patient relationship in a nutshell.

The artist's personal background, biography, cultural heritage, and lived experience are incorporated into their pieces. The works are individual testimonies and social-political critiques as well as meditations on broad human situations. This personal grounding lends authenticity and specificity to the artworks enabling them to resonate in a broad social and cultural dialogue opening them to multiple readings that enrich the artwork's relevance and impact. With changes of scale, theme, and technique, viewers come into a direct, relationship with figurative artworks, reflecting the complex identity and social landscape of the era.

# At The Millennium's End

## Small Figurative Artwork in the United States

# *Perplexed*

This bronze sculpture effectively conveys the interconnected concepts of technical proficiency and emotional expression. Its pose, arms flat at the sides, head just barely tilted to one side, creates a sense of quiet introspection, of perplexity, that brings the sculpture beyond mere representation. The sense of perplexity is clear and emotional. It reads powerful, almost hushed, a state of stillness, a moment frozen, a state of interior thought that the viewer is encouraged to follow. It is more often associated with large-scale and monumental sculpture's grandiose nature. This level of emotional nuance, of restraint, and delicacy of mood, can be difficult to bring out in smaller-scale works. The finely detailed musculature, careful attention to proportions, and bodily movements suggest a comprehensive study of the human form. The choice to leave the figure unclothed continues to emphasize shape and structure, as well as a raw vulnerability. The surface of the body gives a sense of energy and essence to the sculpture breathing life into the form on a sensory level. This becomes an evolving conversation between artist, material, and viewer, inviting a dialogue of scale and thought.

**Artist Statement - 1998**

My work explores the human body, depicting real people with real bodies in quiet, private moments. They have the imperfections we all have, a little too much or too little here and there. I never idealize the bodies I sculpt because every muscle and roll of fat has something to communicate. People's life experiences shape their bodies and the shape of their bodies reflects those experiences. Each piece is a celebration of the human condition in a way that is quiet, commonplace, and universal.

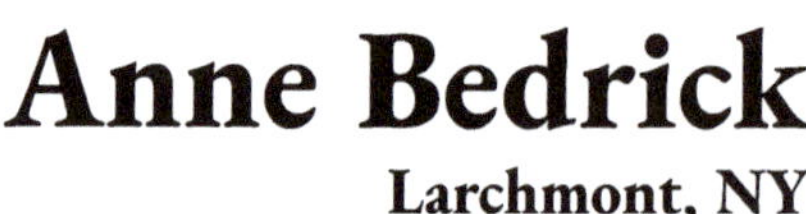

## Anne Bedrick

**Larchmont, NY**

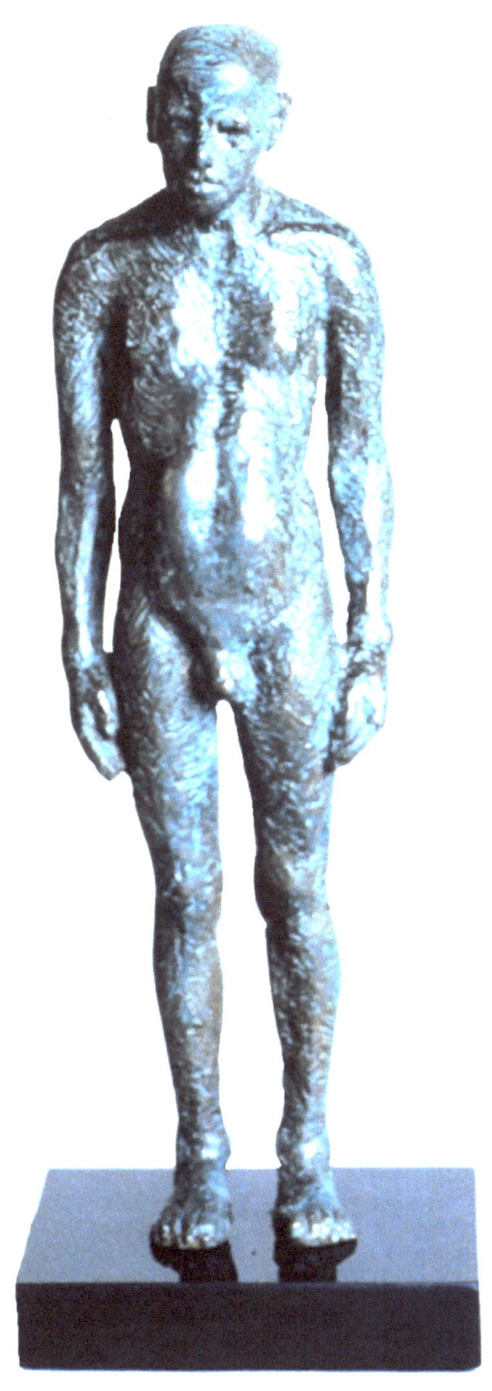

***Perplexed***
bonded bronze
11 x 3 x 2

# *Independent Ego*

*Independent Ego* is a 3D mixed media rectangular metal framed sculpture visibly bordered with screws. Inside the frame, there is a sculptural composition of a human-like figure entangled in an intricate arrangement. The figure in the center of the composition, with its legs and ribcage in a fetal huddle, is a strong focal point, with body posture and coloration working together to create a sense of vulnerability, isolation, and perhaps a desire for protection in this inhospitable environment. The wrapping cables and tubular forms are visually and conceptually compelling, as they obliterate the line between body and machine, flesh and conduit, so that the viewer considers themes of dependency, limitation, and how technology becomes absorbed in our identities. Wrapping cables and tubular forms are visually and conceptually compelling, suggesting some control or subjugation is exerted upon the figure. Multiple interpretations are possible through this merging of materials and ideas to engage viewers in mindfulness. The title, *Independent Ego*, adds to this interactive environment. Is the ego truly independent, or is it our imagination?

**Artist Statement - 1998**

LEADER: I am empowered. I make my life decisions without thought of others. I alone created the vacuum in which I exist. I control my emotions, thoughts, and experiences. I am my own master.

GROUP: You really are a self-centered selfish bastard aren't you?

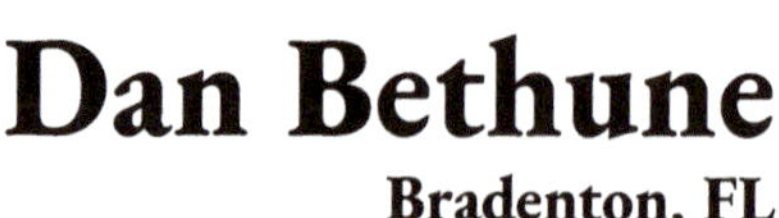

**Dan Bethune**

**Bradenton, FL**

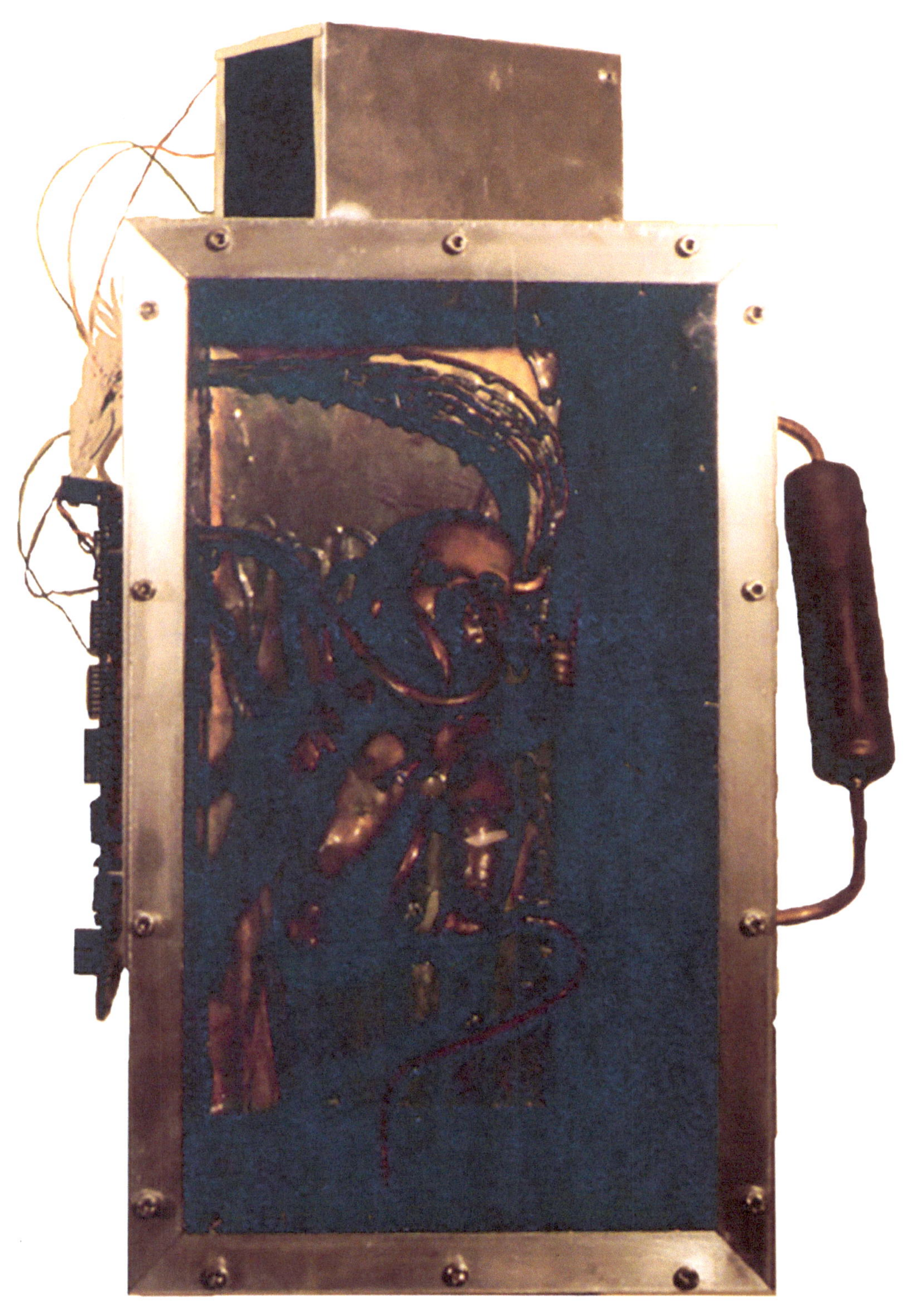

***Independent Ego***
mixed media
16 x 12

# *Legs Up I*

**Legs Up I starts out with a bold red backdrop, and that's the first thing that grabs you. A figure lying on its back with legs up and organic vertical forms to the left has an abstract awkwardness. The left forms with its range of green and grey colors speaks of a depth, fluidity, and a textured surface, a growing of something organic, impermanent, or eroding in real time. The two raised legs on the right are primarily made up of golden yellow hues. The contrast between the luminous red and the earthier textures of the legs compels a spectator to absorb and examine how colors interact with texture. The dark vertical accents included within it bring a coarser texture and an apparent touchability to this abstract centerpiece, giving a more visual interest for viewer engagement. There is a nice play with light and dark, soft and harsh textured surfaces, muted and bright colors in these spaces that show consideration for composition and materiality. This abstract figurative piece has a state of tension, balance, curiosity, and thoughtfulness.**

**Artist Statement - 1998**

Looking at and painting the model is really a way of seeing oneself. For me, the model is both a window and a mirror. As I look out at the subject I become one with it. Then the figure as subject becomes both her or himself and me. One's work is ultimately about oneself. (My) paintings appear in collections throughout the United States and Europe. Six summers have been spent in Assisi, Italy, where the people, as well as the architecture, have been an inspiration. My work always returns to people and places. This is true even in its most abstract form where the place is inside me.

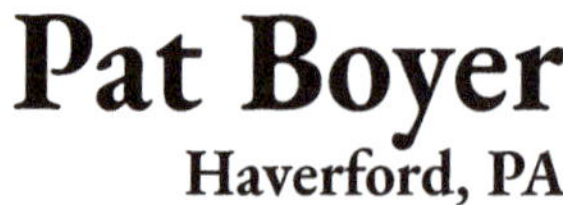


**Haverford, PA**

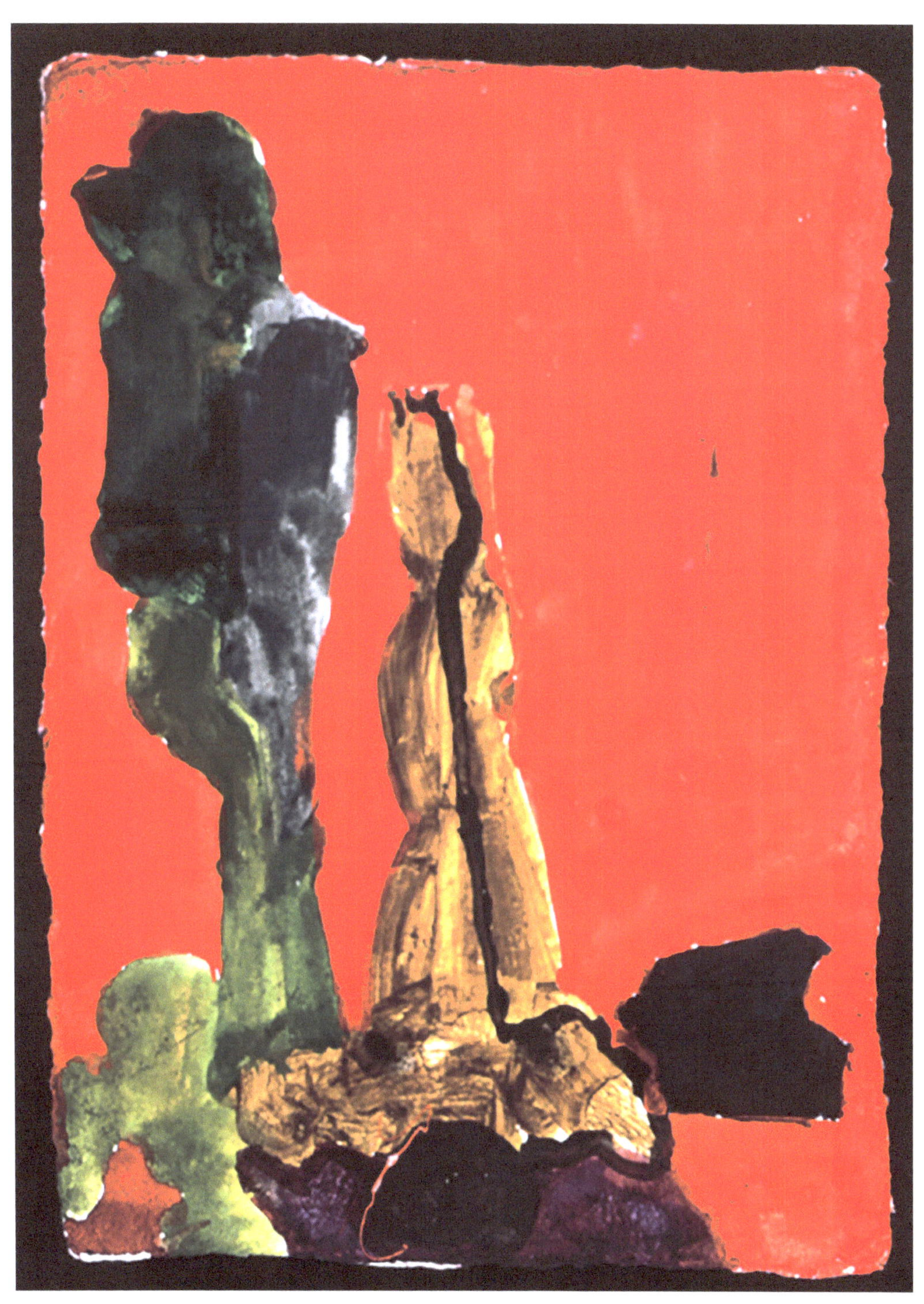

***Legs Up I***
Water Media
on Handmade Paper
11 x 9

# *Offering*

Offering is a mixed medium and ceramic image of the figure with what appears to be a human head peering deliberately out of an elongated, brown cloaked form that runs vertically up the body in the center. In the middle of this brown cloak is a bright red ladybug resting in small white hands on an earth colored coat. Those ladybug holding hands offer a tender point of tension with framing that resonates with ideas of fragility, potential promise, or change. The pastel coloured, granular light beige and soft white background contrasts to draw emphasis onto the central image of a character with its muted tone and understated symbolism, giving it a worn appearance. The surface is weathered and maintains a formal frame around the figure, adding an overall ancient appearance, as something that has just been dug up or rediscovered from many centuries ago. The visual texture of the ceramic adds layer and depth to its story. Viewers can contemplate the passage of time and its impact on the human condition. The piece as a whole has an air of mystery and pensiveness, with dark contrasts and textures used to form this contemplative, unified composition rich in symbolism.

**Artist Statement - 1998**

I did a piece once called, "Do You See What I'm Saying?" - an absurd statement if you think about it. But my work is evidence of conversations with myself, something like a visual transcript. The process, as with most anything, is of primary importance. I would hope that process continues as people approach my work. Each visit should bring enlightenment according to individual experience.

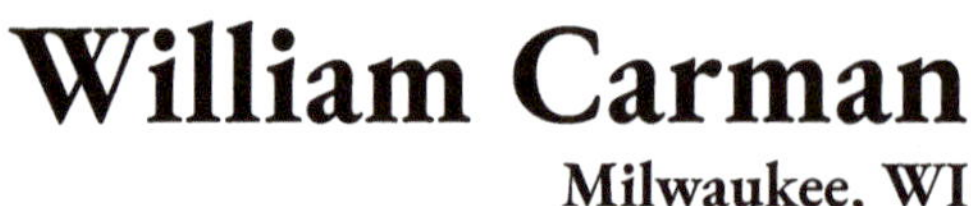


**Milwaukee, WI**

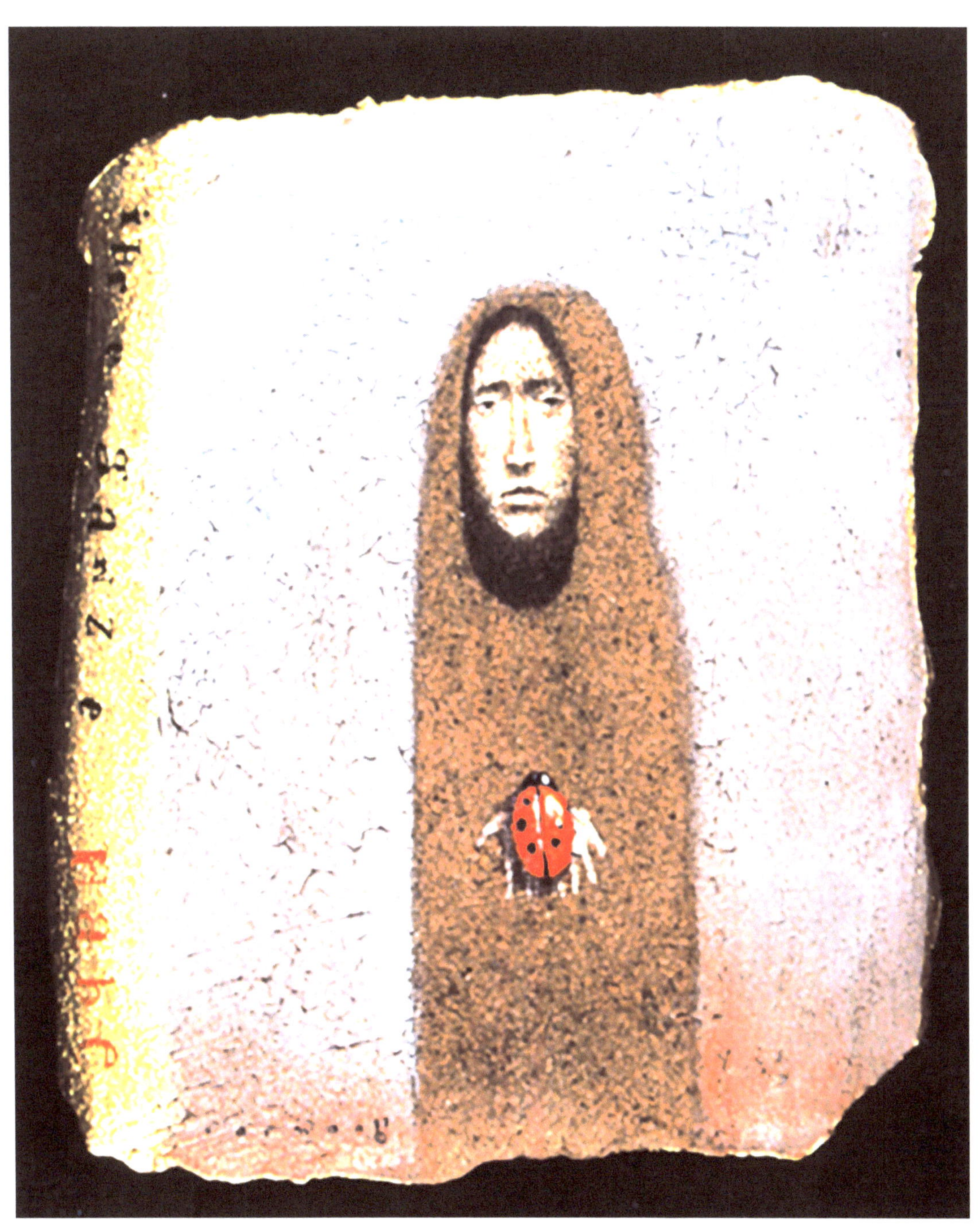


Offering
mixed n ceramic
3 3/4 x3 1/4

# *Rehbok*

*Rehbok* is a bronze sculpture of a doe nursing her fawn. The mother's head lowered protectively over her nursing fawn, showing the care and attention that immerses you in a tranquil bond between mother and child. The long, thin legs emphasize the delicate nature of the bodies themselves and, by extension, this powerful moment. The choice of the artist to zero in on such a small, commonplace aspect of the natural world shows an admiration for the incidentals inherent in subtle and emotive. This small sculpture used organic shaping and gesture to tell its story. In this way, the emotional content between a mother and child is able to come out in an organic fashion, demonstrating how small moments can deliver universal impact.

**Artist Statement - 1998**

In my creations I attempt to depict the essence of the subject matter and bring to the viewer a unique and intimate experience to which the individual can relate and be enmeshed without being insulted or overwhelmed. I capture a fleeting gesture of life and freeze it for posterity. My works are aimed to lift the human spirit and promote happiness by bringing the human experience to a plan of dignity and decency. This reminds us that the proper study of mankind is more than man. My themes are universal and although outwardly secular, they evoke spiritual nuances. The coldness of metal is transformed into a warm and boundless experience which helps the viewer escape into serenity away from the preoccupations of ordinary life. If nothing else, they should stimulate old memories and assuage the unconscious emptiness in us all by enriching the visible qualities of our everyday environment.

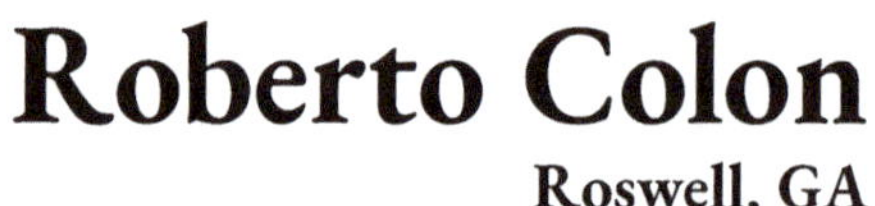

## Roberto Colon

**Roswell, GA**

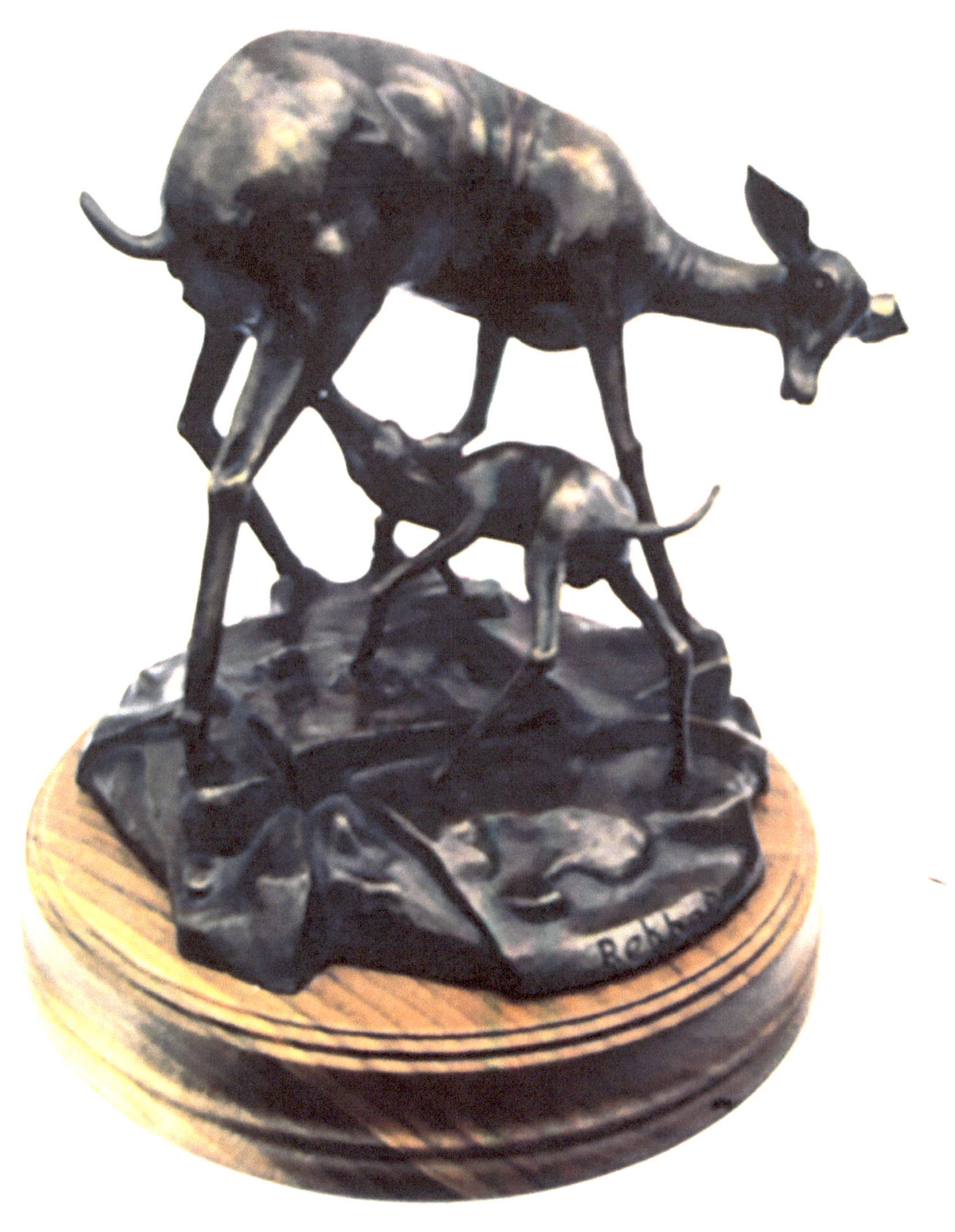

***Rehbok***
Bronze
10 x 13 x 9

# *Floating Field*

A Polaroid emulsion transfer nude on watercolor paper of a woman with a slightly bowed head turned down and a bit to the side, with her eyes closed, and a tranquil or reflective look on her face. The translucent Polaroid emulsion transforms into a liquid cloth-like fold that encases her, offering movement distending along the body, acting like a fabric with dark organic and mineral hues, which clash with her radiant skin; underscored by the soft lighting that emphasizes her silhouette. The white on white backdrop highlights the mysterious figure and soft interplay of shadow & light in its movement on her body and the fabric. The composition is both fragile and graceful with an airiness that keeps the portrait expressing tension, vulnerability, and elegance.

**Artist Statement - 1998**

There is an inherent paradox in Danny Conant's photographs. Her figures, mostly nudes, are at once corporeal and spiritual, seemingly rooted in a mythological past, yet very much of the here and now. From a distance, the muted, earthy tones of these pictures and their sculpted forms convey serenity, elegance, and grace. A viewer, allured by the sheer sensuality of the image, is upon closer inspection confronted with an intimacy and intensity that can be disquieting. These figures aren't posed, they're captured, transformed, and transported, out of one moment, into another. Employing the most experimental of emulsion lift techniques the silken textures and hand-rendered effects she achieves on watercolor paper are her own signature.

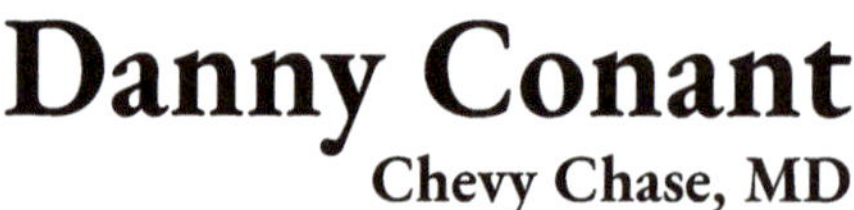

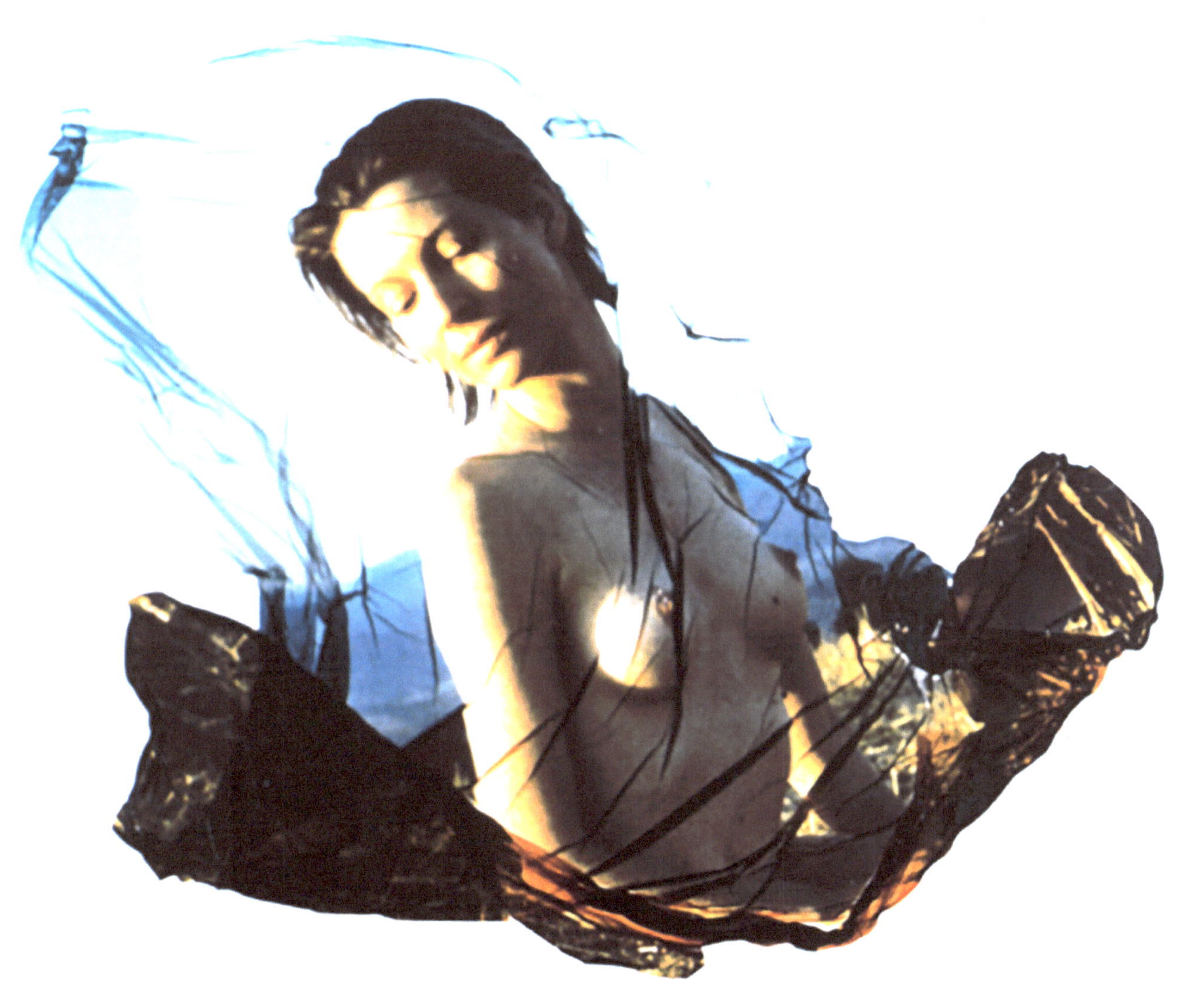

***Floating Field***
Emulsion transfer on
watercolor paper
8 x 10

# *Introspection I*

The bronze sculpture, *Introspection I* immediately impresses with a dynamic, contorted pose full of energy and tension. The limbs are bent and intertwined, with one arm reaching upward and the other arm crossing the body. The legs are bent at the knees, creating a sense of tension and movement. The pose itself is an effective device for engaging the viewer: the upward reach of one arm juxtaposed with the defensively crossed other limb creates a tension that feels both physical and metaphorical. This interplay between movement and restraint draws the eye around the sculpture, encouraging it to be viewed from multiple angles. The bent knees and twisted torso further enhance this sense of motion, refusing any sense of static repose and instead suggests the ongoing effort and resilience required to hold such a position. The anatomy reflects the strain and imperfection of this arduous pose, creating an honest, almost raw depiction of human determination. Ultimately, the piece's uniqueness emerges from a commitment to capturing not just the appearance of human strength and endurance, but the very sensation of it. A testament to the perseverance intrinsic in the human spirit.

**Artist Statement - 1998**

A language that speaks visually through the senses is what I am searching for. There is much to observe and much to be said. Reconnect us with the natural rhythms, cycles. Seek the rapture of being alive. It's not lost.

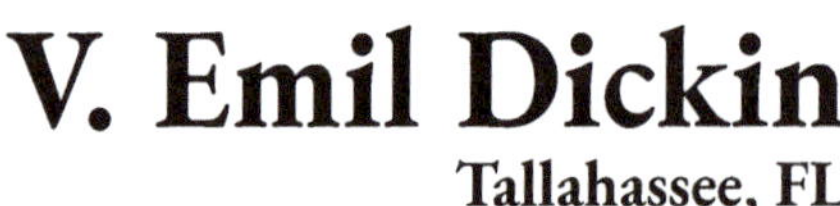

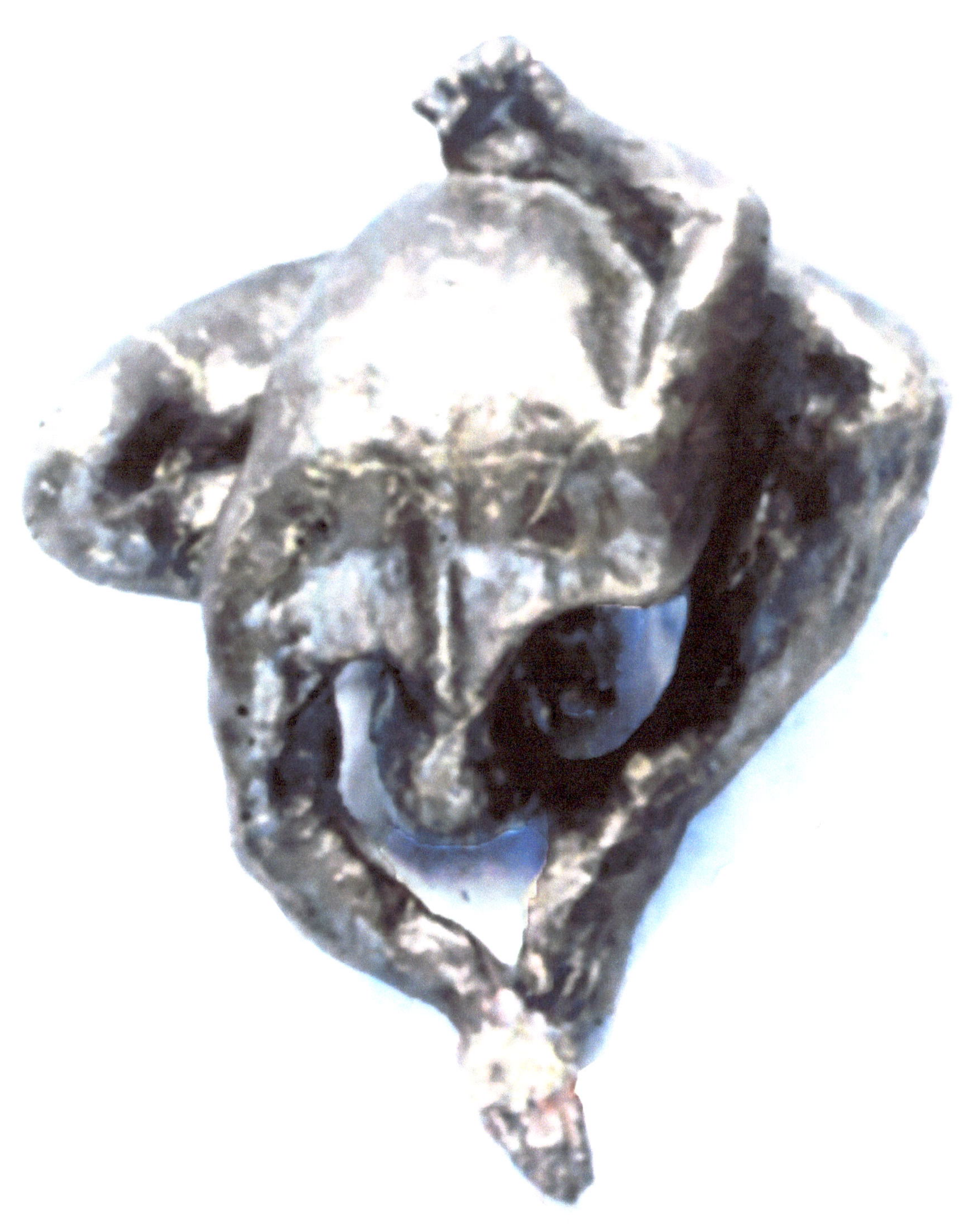

***Introspection I***
Bronze
9 x 7 x 4

# *Untitled*

The painting *Untitled*, demonstrates a confident command of the figure, employing expressive, textured brushstrokes that communicate both the weight and suppleness of the reclining body, stripping away unnecessary detail and focusing on the basic essence of the human figure. Situated between expressionism and realism, and allowing an emotional, intimate moment of the figure emerges naturally. The lighting gives prominence to a natural reclining body and the tension in the pose. The way the fingers splay across the torso is a suggestive detail, infusing the composition with a sense of vulnerability and self-possession. The geometric patterns of the floorboards' beneath the body provide a visual grounding as well as a compositional counterpoint to the organic shapes of the man's flesh, adding both depth and the sense of space to the painting.

**Artist Statement - 1998**

I base this work on my personal relationships that I develop between myself and my sitters, attempting to capture and portray each subject in a state of both beauty and vulgarity, strength and fragility, and awkwardness and self-possession. It is in this flux of character that I find a true sense of emotion and expression. I construct my figures and narratives through the seductive nature of paint, building the layers of marks so that each one becomes a specific shape and color of the whole, in order to promote the same complexities in the surface of the painting as in the subject. My application of brush marks responds to the subject and captures intuitively the essence of form. The painting itself embodies the ambiguity between ingenuity and awareness, making form and content work together.

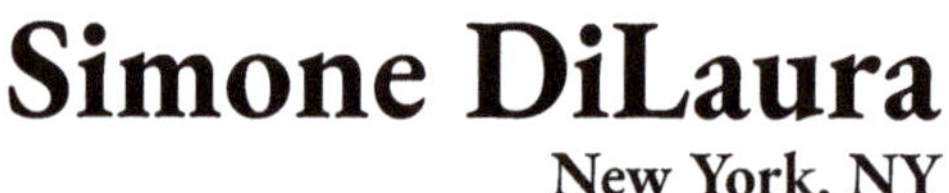

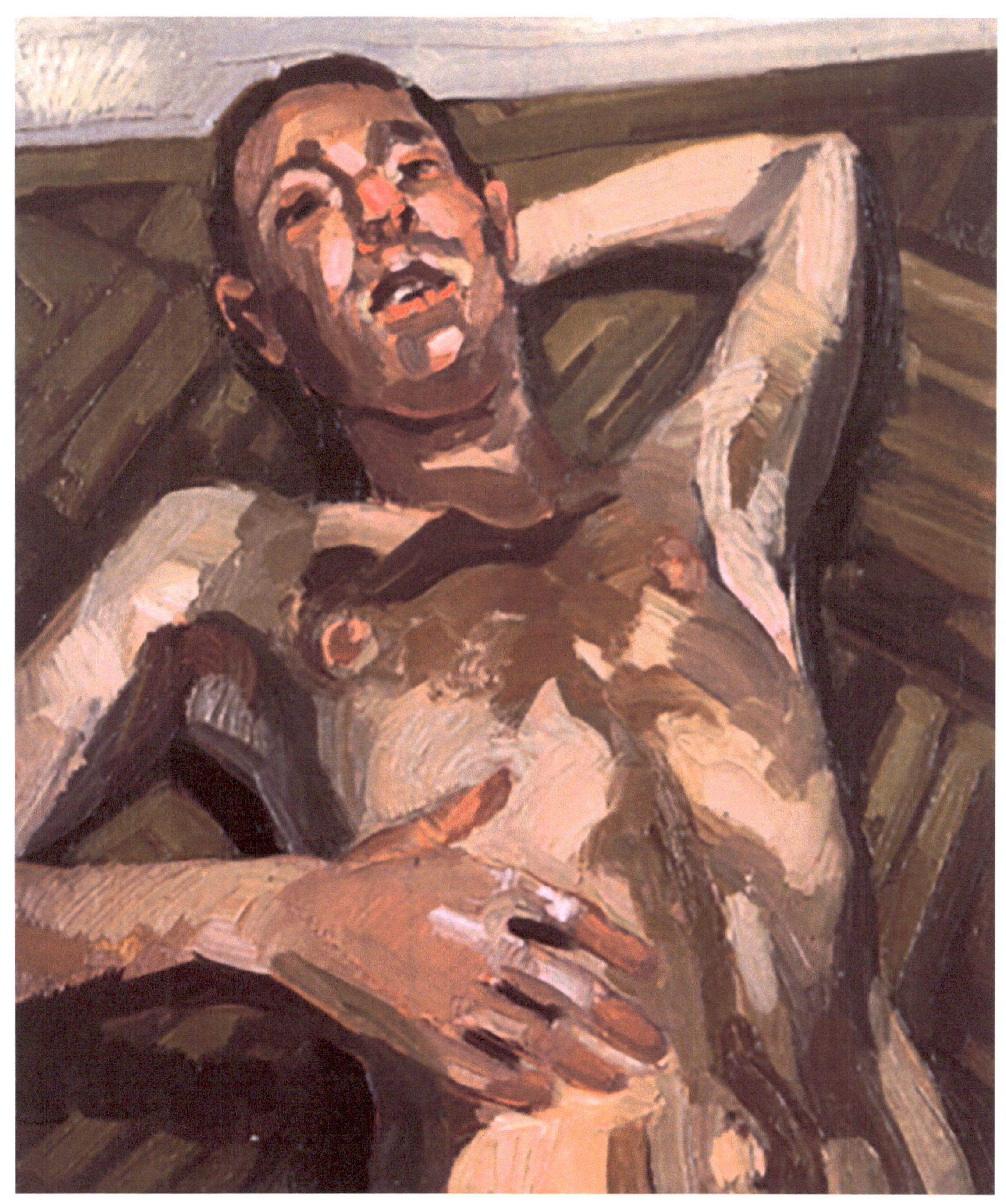

***Untitled***
oil on linen
8 x 9

# *Epitaph for a Sun Watcher*

Perhaps the most abstract figurative work discussed here. The pelvic suggestion through the decision to split a circle into two visually distinct halves. This tension immediately initiates a contemplation of balance, division, and harmony, creating a narrative that hints at both contemporary and ancient explorations of contrast and duality in stories, and share experiences. The piece evokes a meditation on the relationship between the human-made and the natural. The bold, solid black left half offers a sense of visual weight and stability, establishing a clear geometric presence. The right half's wooden-like organic trace with grain and irregular edges, introduces vulnerability that counterbalances the austerity of the black form. This engages the viewer in a dynamic conversation of the human condition through an abstract perspection.

**Artist Statement - 1998**

The hurricane had strafed the pinelands.
The naked remains became a mother's womb exposed.

The day of the solar eclipse
I found the trees removed like
carcasses,
But for a
half-moon slab,
Revealing
Nature's pelvis, fore and aft,
Umbilical places, in urn and an ode.

A thousand years ago in a desert valley
A watcher listened to the sun
Pick its way across a spiral chord,
and strum the cycles
of heavenly bodies upon a rock.

## Richard Duncan

**Miami, FL**

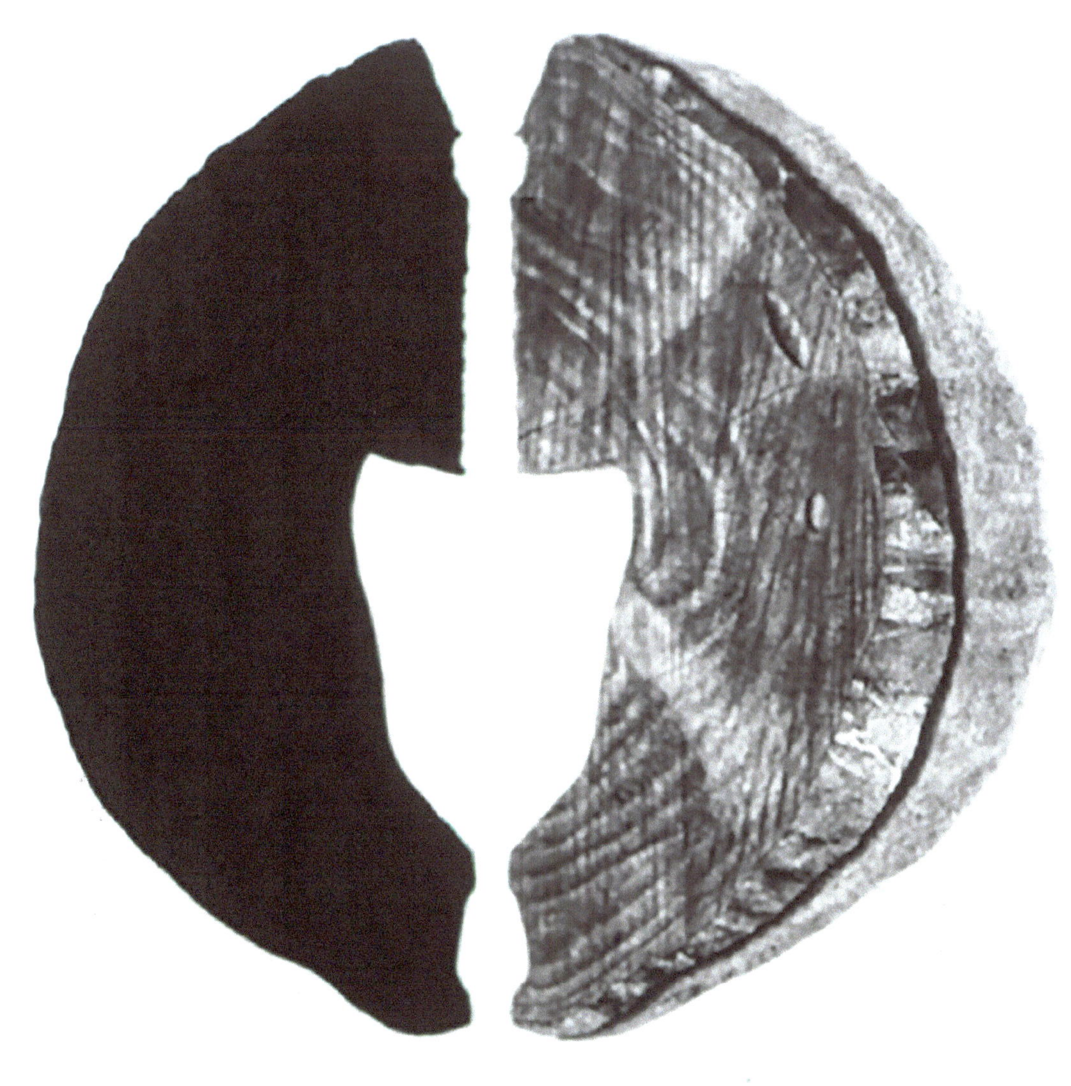

*Epitaph for a Sun Watcher*
etching
12x12

# *Amelia Series #6*

Painted in a free and expressive manner with thick, textured brushstrokes, the portrait is a declaration of its bold manipulation of warm and cool color decisions that demand attention from the viewer. The painting process gives this piece a lot of movement and energy with broad textured strokes. These rough brush strokes build an emotionality in the portrait, with sincerity and urgency that embraces both an energetic brutality and emotional honesty. The closed eyes are a nice touch that encapsulates the situational image and is reflective at the same time. The piece is imbued with a quiet, contemplative mood, sharing in a private moment of reflection, evoking emotion through suggestion and texture rather than explicit detail. This gives the work a universal, almost archetypal quality, opening it to personal interpretation.

**Artist Statement - 1998**

*Amelia Series #6* is the sixth work in a series of a hundred studies of my wife in acrylic on masonite. In this painting, I have used rapid brush work to capture the gesture and expression of Amelia. The intense depth of color and shadows work emotions of sensuality. The expressive brush strokes give homage to two Dutch artists Frans Hals and Williem deKooning. It celebrates the portrait work of my Dutch heritage.

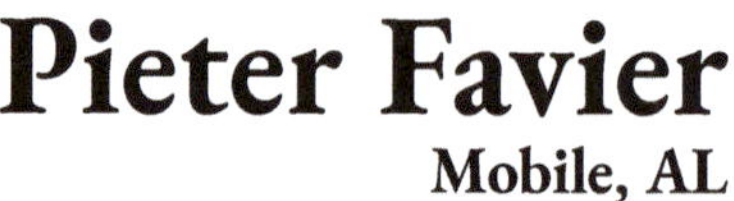

**Pieter Favier**

**Mobile, AL**

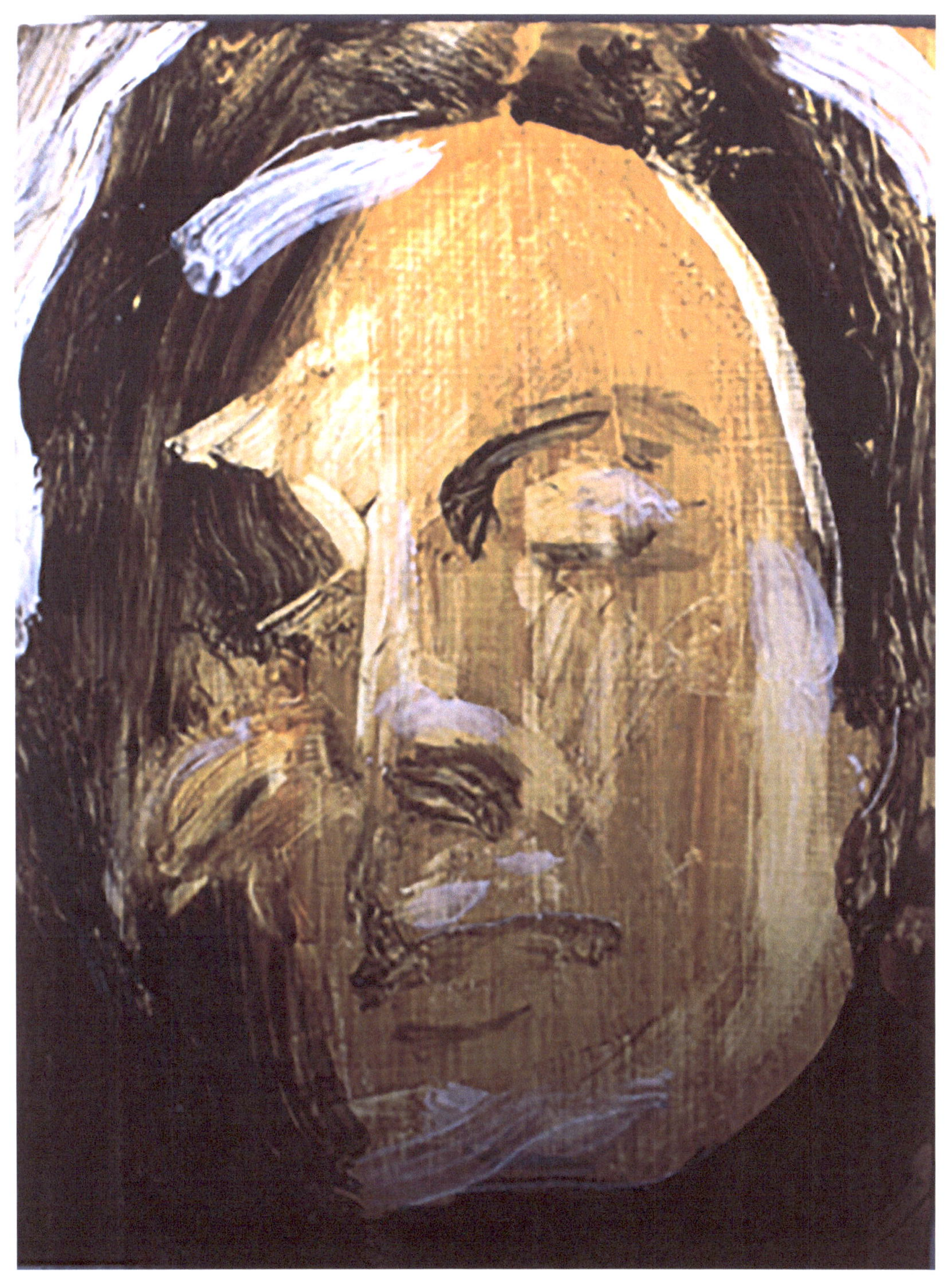

***Amelia Series #6***
Acrylic on masonite
15 1/2 x 12

# *Mother and Jacob*

**The painting has an intimate look at shared human experience that falls somewhere between abstraction and figuration. The figures are not too specifically defined, but with enough detail to retain an emotional accuracy that reaches beyond realism. Both abstract and expressive, the figures provide a common ground upon which viewers can project feelings about care, vulnerability, and protection. The intermittent golden lines function both as a visual frame to introduce depth to the composition, but are also symbolic in the boldness of their use, and hint at stained glass with a Madonna and child theme; a signifier representing all that connects us energy-wise, which we can not see between people. The painting has a rhythm, giving the scene pace and energy without taking away from the intimacy.**

**Artist Statement - 1998**

This painting came to me after seeing my mother and my nephew in a Christmas pageant in Ivyland, PA. Seeing them in their costumes, watching my four year old nephew struggle and squirm while my mother endured putting on his clothes, gave me a sense that I was seeing something timeless. I had not just witnessed my mother's maternal care over my nephew, but how my childhood must have been and the generations of childhood before us. In this particular case when I decided to paint them, I saw the subjects as timeless.

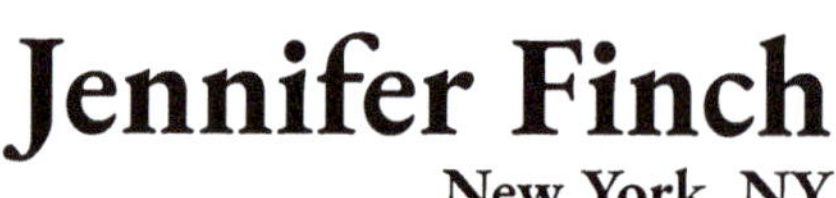

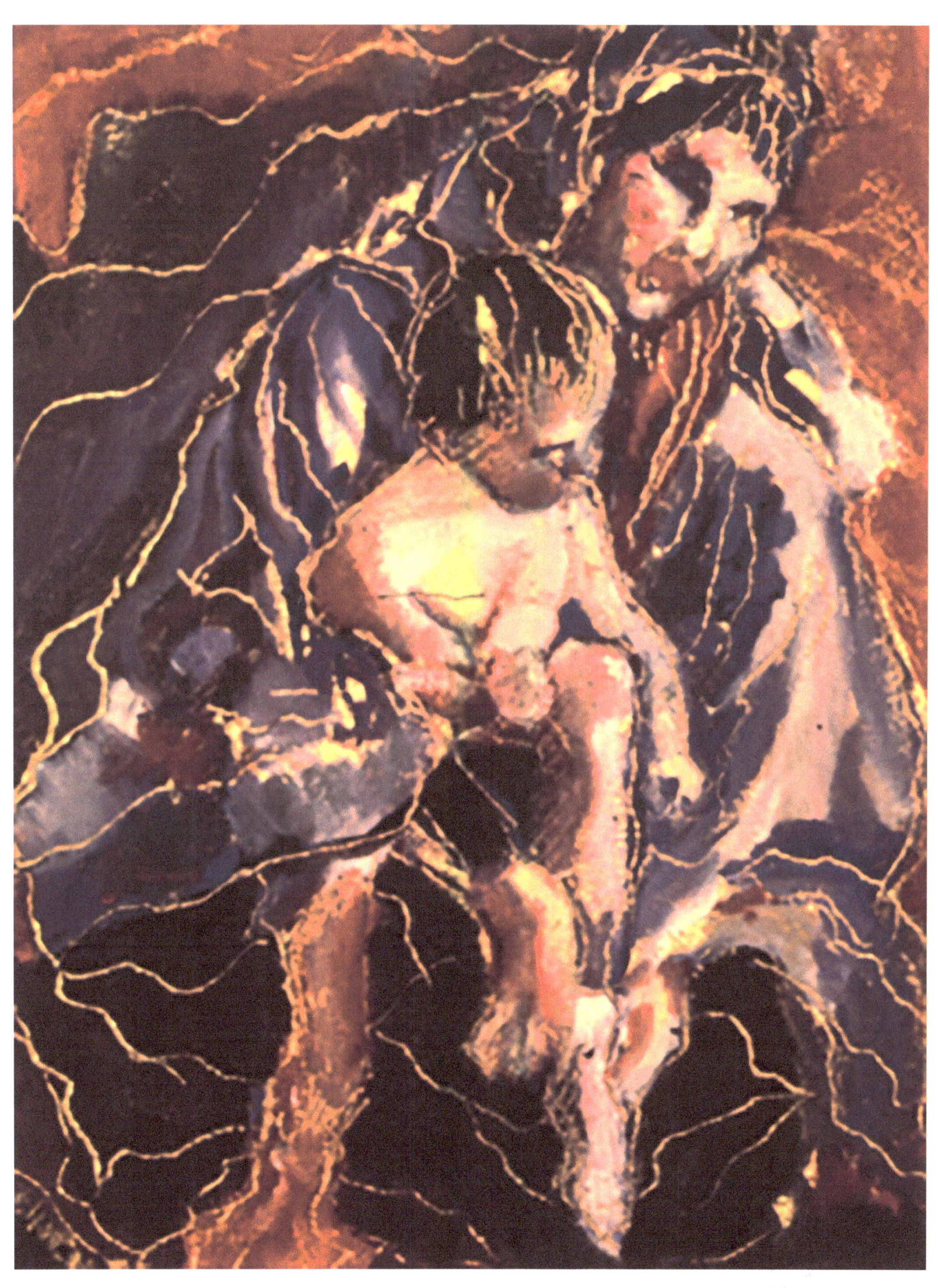

***Mother and Jacob***
oil and enamel on canvas
12x10

## *It's Obvious*

An intriguing and surreal anthropomorphic figure reminiscent of a vintage television is a clever look to both past technology and the idea of observing or remembering, giving the work a sense of timelessness. Two bright yellow chicken figures are positioned at the forefront of the frame and serve as a narrative which viewers may interpret in myriad ways, questions of companionship, confrontation, or shared experience arise, talking back and forth, and listening. The anthropomorphic addition of human arms and legs transforms the artwork into a peculiar, almost puppet-like abstract figure, creating a thought-provoking tension between playfulness and introspection, standing out in its inventiveness and skilled composition. As an example, the directness of the phase, *She Always Listened*, can be read as gentle and supportive, yet also invites questions about what she heard. Did she always listen? Is it obvious? The choices here offer much for viewers to contemplate.

**Artist Statement - 1998**

device bundles snare
cheap
proverbs
discipline level

charm
addiction sale
languid-apparatus

tacky lasso
phases
waspish attitude
elemental
resonate docile
slicker

slumped posture

covet
tame bad myth
goot
courteous remark fatigue lightly
tantalizing
flooded & weak pondering

vanitas stringent
mojo monument

words

# Paige Forshay-Rodefer

**Winston-Salem, NC**

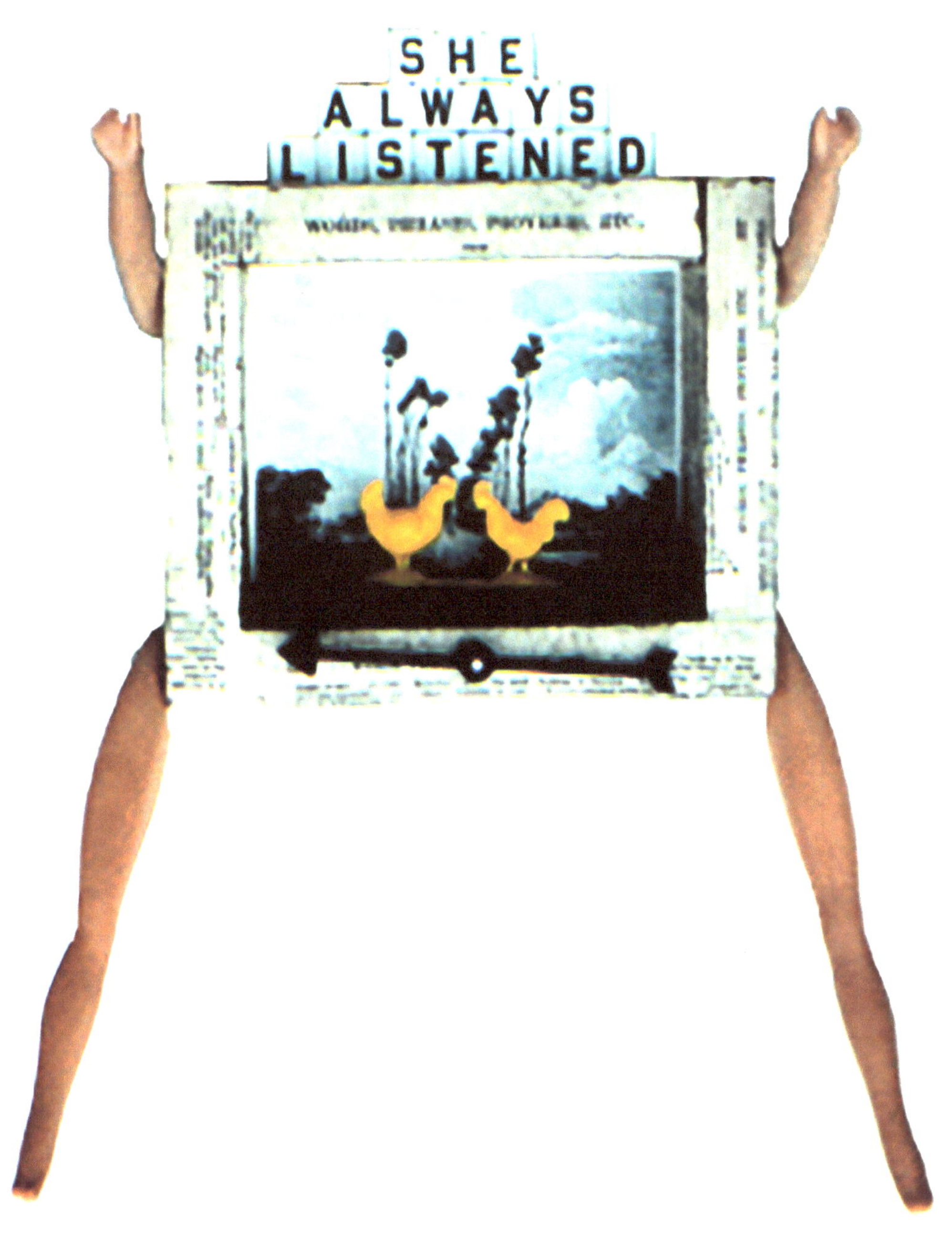


***It's Obvious***
Wood, plastic, mixed media
12 x 7 1/2 x 2

# *Woman at Table*

Woman at Table is an oil-on-canvas painting that renders a complex visual conversation between figuration and abstraction, demarcating the image of a faceless, nude woman in opposition to an abstract colorfield landscape. The figure hovers between planes of similar flat color blocks, functioning as both object and affect with psychological or emotional boundaries in modern and minimalist traditions. This sense of anonymity that the facelessness of the subject creates is powerful; it allows for multiple emotional interpretations, giving a universal element that many viewers can relate to. The painting excels in a bold and powerful composition, beautifully handled, both with subtlety and strength of color and value that provides an emotional impact. A feeling of aloneness or reflection.

**Artist Statement - 1998**

My paintings are about everyday life. Their subjects are mundane and familiar, discovered through the process of painting. In this way, I look for what is taken for granted, unnoticed, so pervasive it has become invisible. My work is akin to an atmosphere, rarely a representation of actuality. "Woman at Table" is no one in particular, yet I recognize in her the woman in the flower shop, my grandmother as a young woman, and even myself.

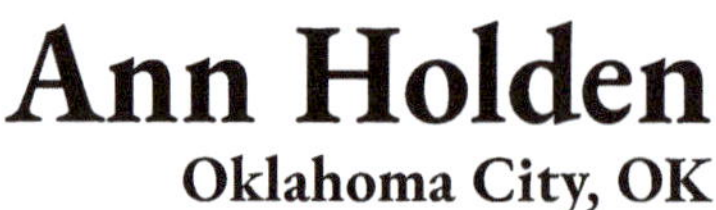


**Oklahoma City, OK**

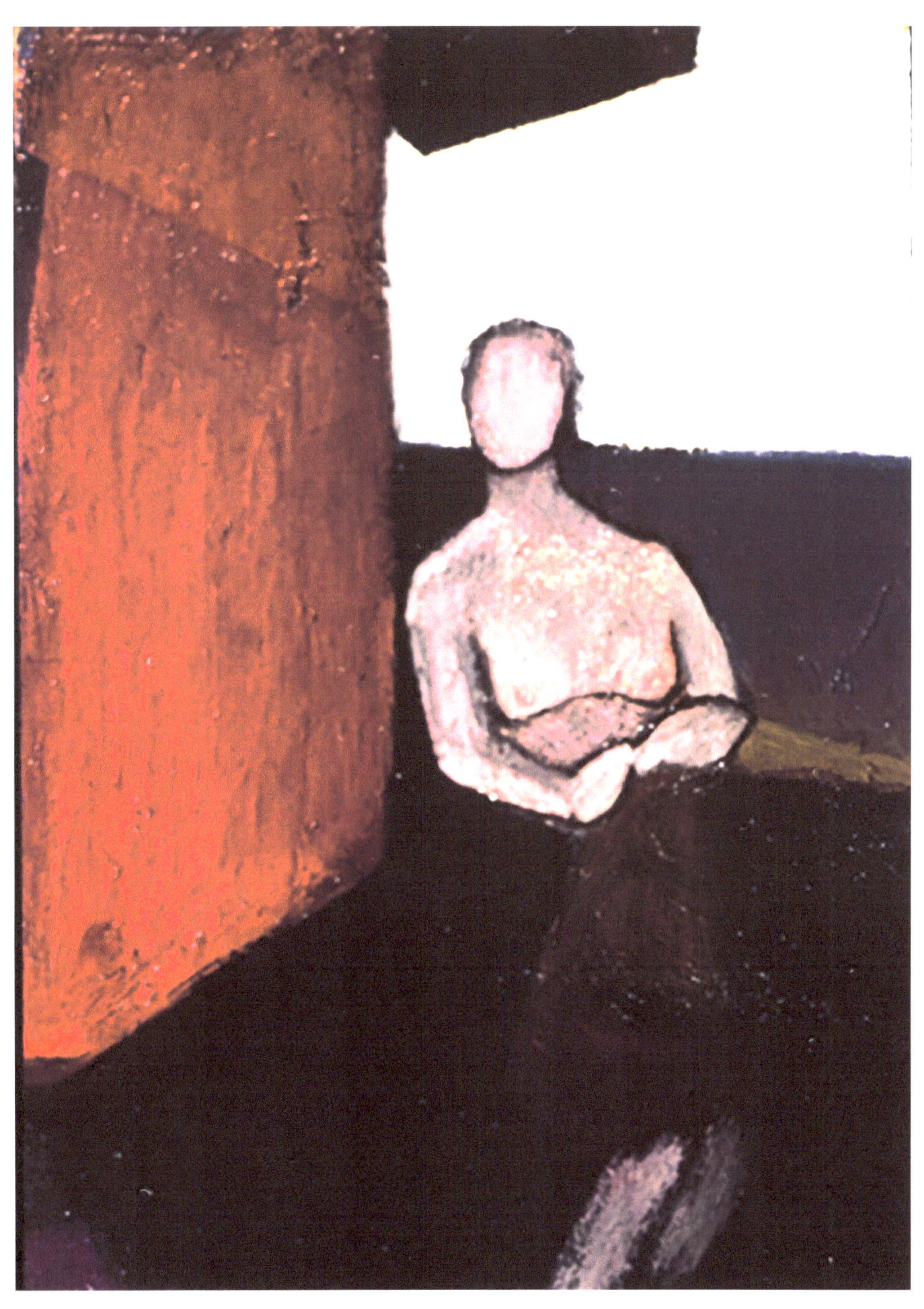

***Woman at Table***
oil on canvas
9x12

# *The Unborn*

A pink-colored sleeveless dress mounted on a designer hanger made of thin silver wire. The top is constructed of a lightweight cotton material, with detailing on it done by hand, like these delicate gold-painted flowers on its right side (left in this pic). Text runs from the upper right to the lower left on the dress. Black tulle is pulled over the front and left side so that colors and images are layered against one another. This piece turns a wearable object into an object of contemplation, simultaneously timeless and personal, offering viewers the opportunity to experience dressing as an act of creation and narrative. The sleeveless dress fulfills the need for art to be emotional, personal, and tactile. The text on the top right suggests a narrative of possible personal significance, and the weaving and xerox transfer onto the design makes an impact. The black tulle, sheer as a veil, adds depth and shadow to the work. This art incites an emotive response, prompting one to reassess the capacity of clothing as both object, metaphor, and meaning in human experience.

**Artist Statement - 1998**

There is a tenuous line between beauty and repulsion, the disturbing and intriguing. My current work involves clothing that is stained and torn, then printed on, beaded, appliqued and stitched. The clothes become metaphors for women, past lives of the never born. Bits of poetry give just enough clues to create questions and intrigue, which allows the viewer to search for elusive answers.

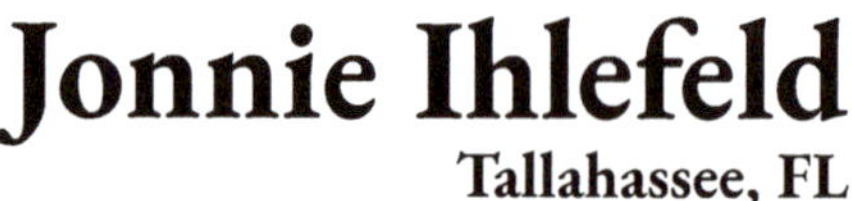

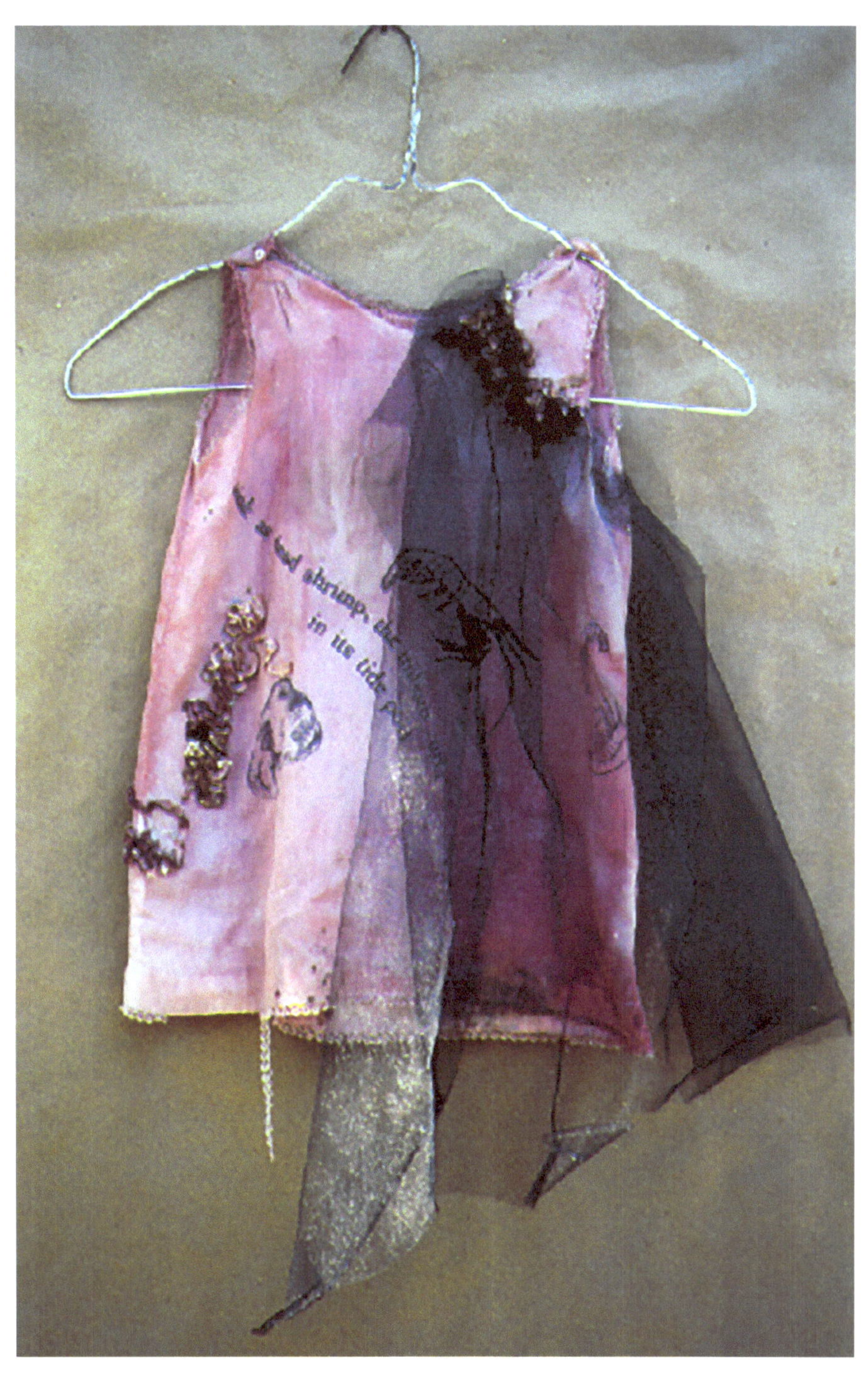


***The Unborn***
Dress dyed, xerox transferred,
appliqued, beaded
12x12x2

# *A Good Egg*

An expressive portrait painted with acrylic, this painting has a strong face full of energy and character with dark hair, a large nose, full lips, and huge green eyes that look away. His red garment is sprinkled with scattered, irregular orange spots. They cradle a shiny, ovoid, pale blue egg in between his thumb and forefinger, near his mouth. The scene has been rendered with a simple, dark purplish background that is painted over a framed board, making the figure and the blue object pop out. With bold colors, and broad brush strokes, this painting provides a feeling of contemplation or internal tension, with emotional accessibility while focusing on the face. His gaze while looking off while holding the blue egg out toward the viewer suggest an invitation to look into his private world, a questioning of the human condition, a mixing of portraiture and psychological experiment. The painting communicates intensity in its pose, its expression, and its surface vibrancy, by stressing mood and character, becomes an ability to communicate feeling.

**Artist Statement - 1998**

i be born from a blue egg
sold from a poor peasant woman
for a bit of cents
the egg held far from a heart
turned to stone long ago
a heart beating from inside the egg
does not stifle its life
for but a dim glimmer of connectedness
within the dark cold clammy hold
of the hand that pulses it away

the egg in all its innocence
hatches itself from the outside in
a soul emerges

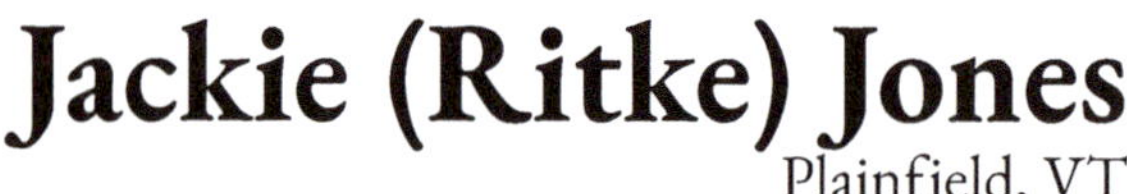


Plainfield, VT

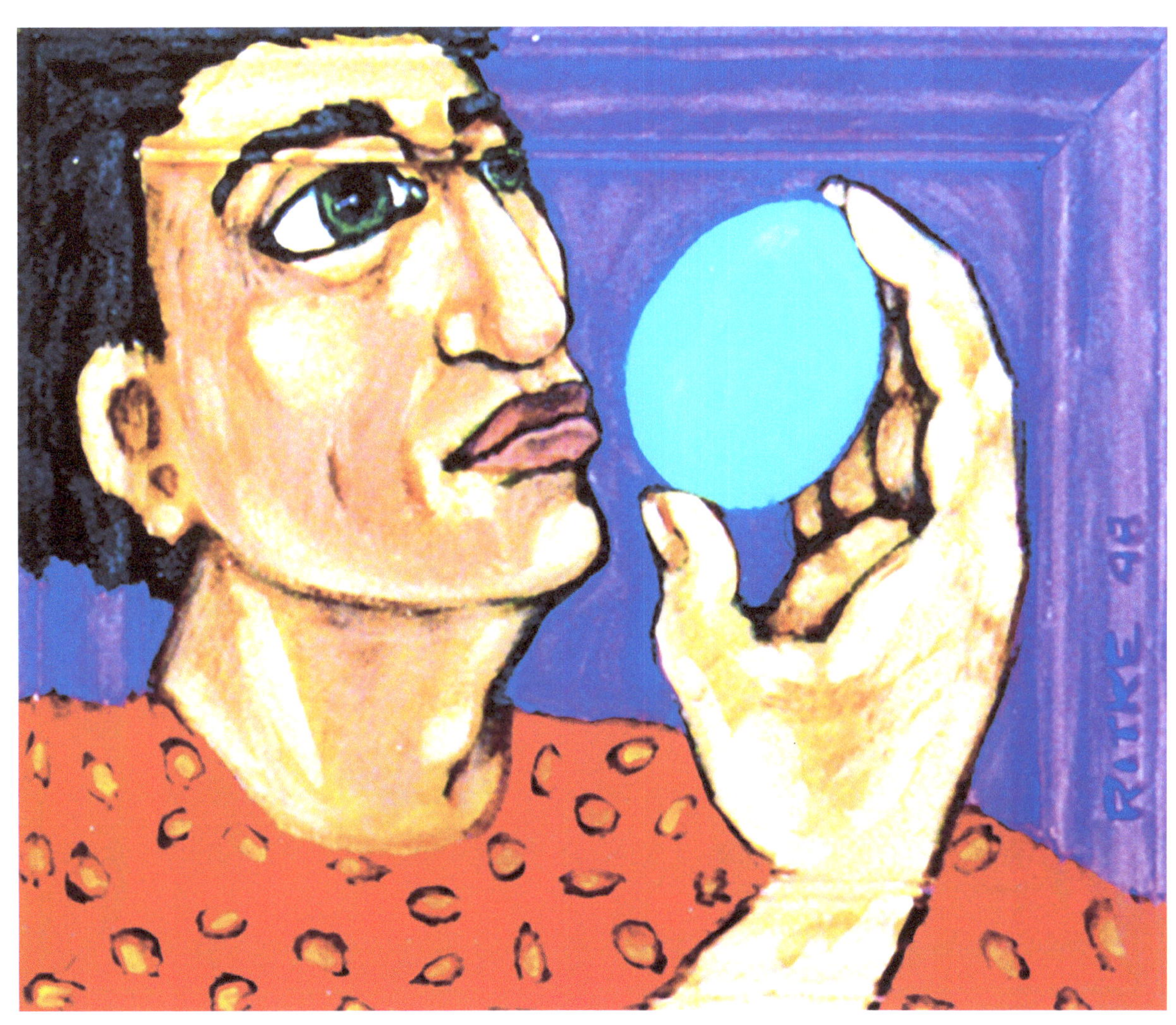

**A Good Egg**
Acrylic on board
with painted frame
10x12

# *The Clearing*

The drawing looks like an old photograph of women in immense skirts, blouses, and hats, and the monochrome dark grey graphite adds to it a timeless feeling. Tree trunks, with their dizzying details, and the focus on the grey sky guide the eyes upwards. These vertical lines initiating movement create a sense of a forest, conveying a feeling rather than color. The complex texture in the drawing reveals light responding in the image through hand-placed dots, and influencing a mood of calm and concentration. The picture captures a moment of quiet between the women and how nature interacts with the figures. This interaction suggests the women have a reflective attitude in a peaceful environment.

**Artist Statement - 1998**

My main body of work consists of drawings, most of which are done in graphite. The figures I choose to portray are family members or neighbors. I enjoy the feel of a landscape while also exploring the relationship of people to each other as well as their connection to the land they choose to live on or near. My subject matter includes a father dancing with his daughters in the back yard, sisters sharing a warm conversation while walking across the lawn, a tree-lined residential street, and a group of women in a clearing in the woods. My drawings tend to resemble old photographs, and the small scale provides an intimate setting which lends itself well to sharing my way of seeing.

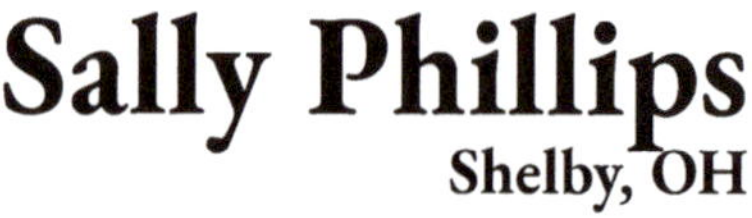

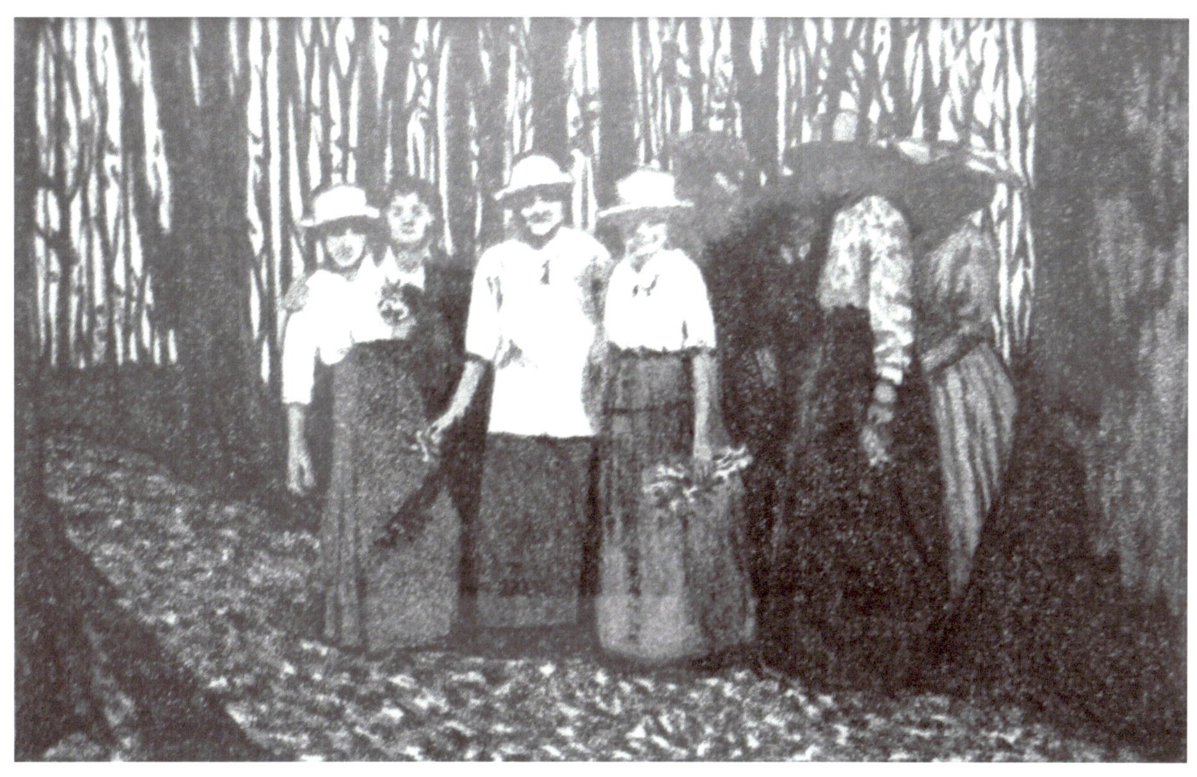

***The Clearing***
Graphite drawing
2 1/2 x 4

# *Too Loose La Trek*

There is a metallic human-like form reminiscent of an android or robot. You can see the joints at the shoulders, elbows, wrists, hips, knees, and ankles are flexible, so it looks like this figure is meant for motion or posing. The serling silver surface reflects a smooth, frictionless aspect. Elongated and stylized with minimal facial features across a thin design the face gives the piece a futuristic, mechanical look, with the high-gloss, reflective finish that gives the piece a mysterious, futuristic quise as the surface gleams and ripples with reflected ambient light. Reflections that dance through its form add volume to the figure even in repose. It is a very clean and minimalist design that captures both machine and anatomical elements in an elegant cohesion with the mirror-like surface flowing around the features. This minimalism leads viewers to think not only of what is there, but also of what has been left out. An understanding of the essentiality and reality of humanity with technology triggers questions on identity, consciousness, and our future evolutionary path.

**Artist Statement - 1998**

My training as an artist and metalsmith is married with my training as a machinist in the creation of this piece.

Too Loose was born out of an exploration of the human body and its potential for manipulation and movement. When someone holds the figure it often takes on the personality of the person holding it.

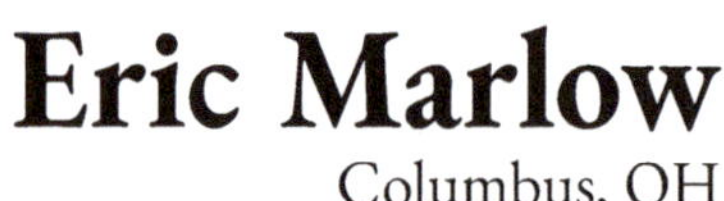


Columbus, OH

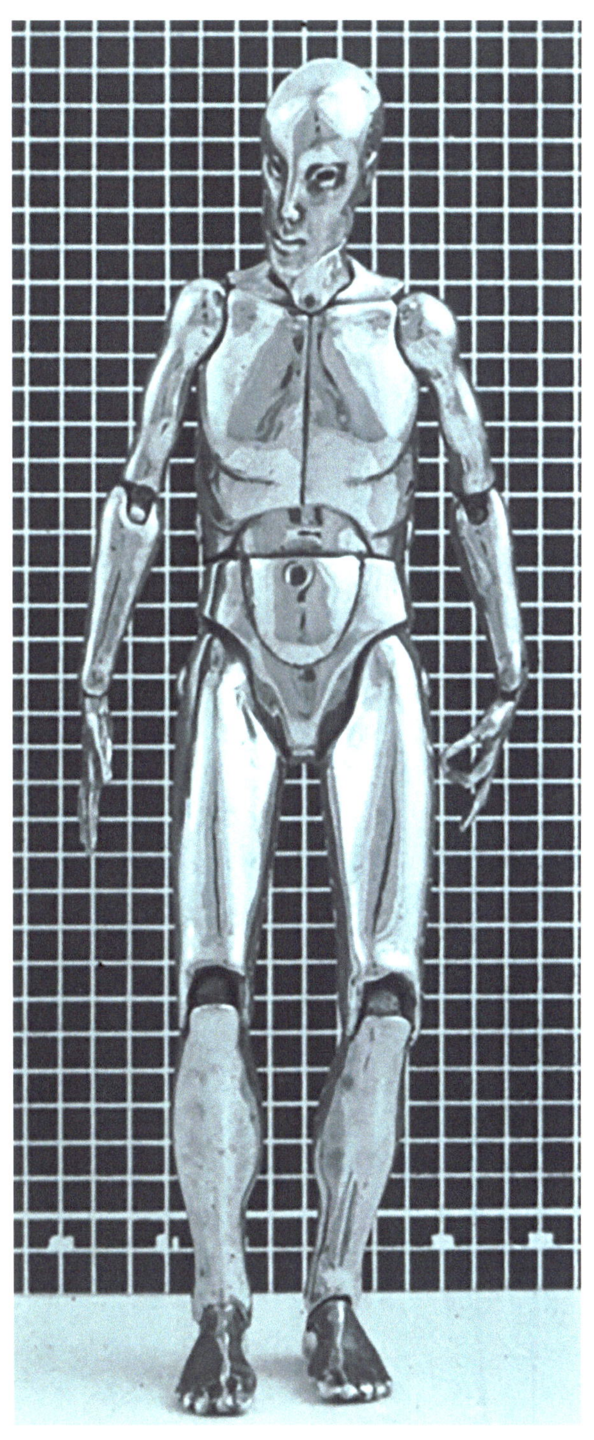

***Too Loose La Trek***
Sterling Silver
6x2x1

## *Catwoman*

**Human and feline features to used to create an innovative figure. A cat's head, with whiskers and pointy little ears, and enormous sci-fi styled eyes. This head interacts with a more humanistic muscle form, creating a dynamic dance between whimsy coupled with power. The sculptures vertical alignment, embellished with a graceful cat tail leaning casually to one side and a possible activity by an object the piece holds, fills the sculptural figure with life. Through an exploration of what this transformation, duality, or perhaps even playfulness can mean for identity, evokes thinking about history, stories, and emotions tied to the hybridity of the cat and woman of this figure. What are women taught in our culture, and subsequently, what roles they perform?**

**Artist Statement - 1998**

This series of dolls examines the adult roles of women that we are taught as children and buy into. The animals represent the natures of women that are then turned into roles that they play. I am trying to poke fun at these prescriptive roles, by showing that these roles are not pretty and cute, but sometimes scary. In examining these roles, I hope that it will cause women to empower themselves. The role of the sexual animal, the concern for beauty that goes beyond physical boundaries into death or attempting to reverse aging, the roles of wife and mother, are all issues that women face every day. Women have historically been equated with nature and animals. Animal characteristics are used in today's society to demean women: the pussy-cat, bunny, and beaver equated with sexuality; the female dog as bitch; a young woman is called a chick. In examining and making fun of these roles I hope that women become aware of the ways in which we fall into the traps set by American society and empower ourselves to be whatever we want to be. I believe in trying to move beyond boundaries and becoming who we really are.

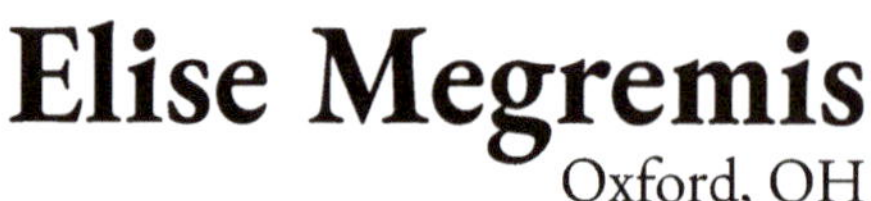

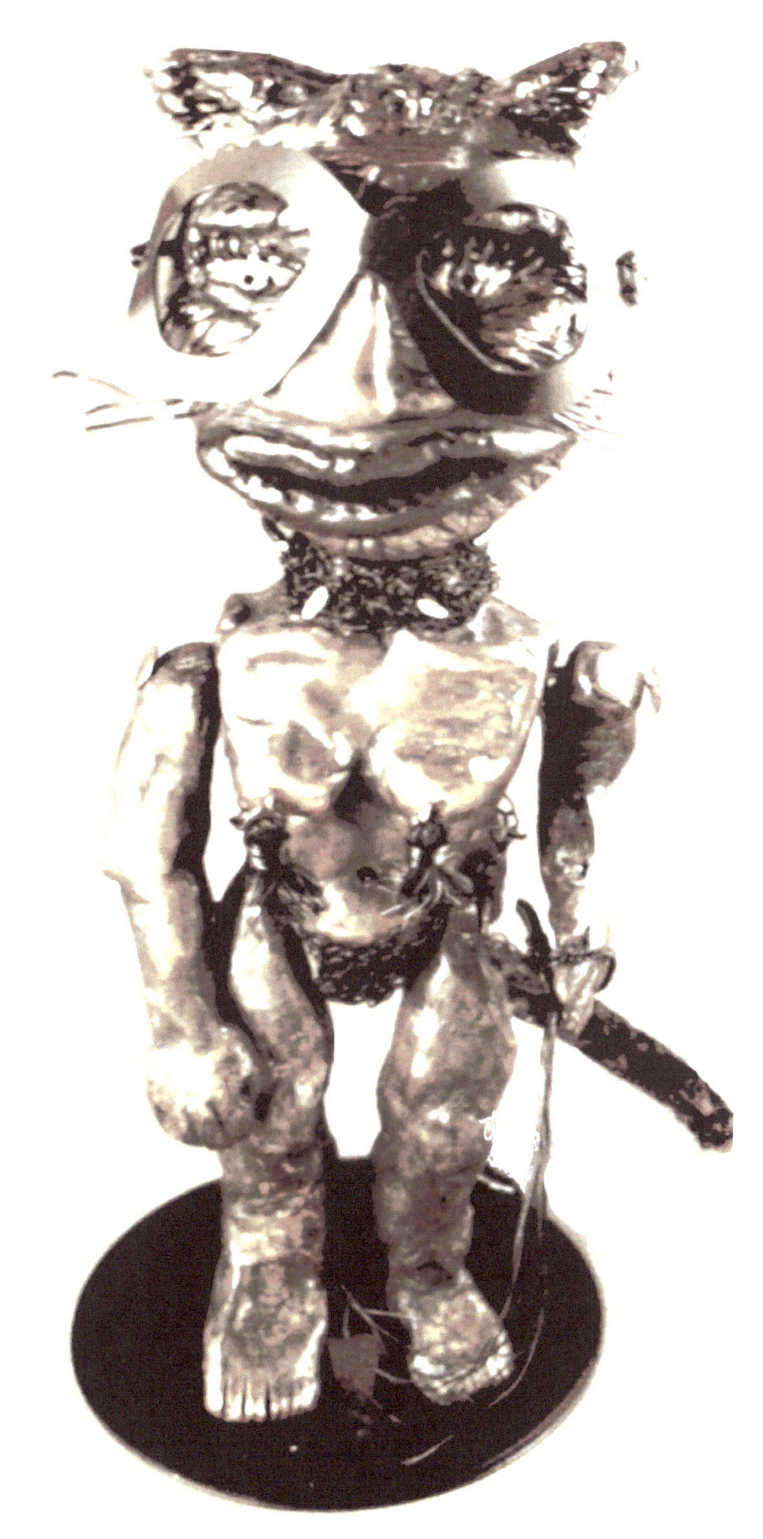

***Catwoman***
Electroformed copper,
copper wire, hair, paint
10x3x2

# *A Tough Nut to Crack*

This sculpture offers an intriguing interpretation of interior room artwork by presenting it within a nutshell. It transforms the room into a dynamic and engaging visual experience. The curvature of the shell enhances a sense of intimacy, as if the space is embracing the viewer, evoking feelings of warmth and comfort associated with the nutshell. Setting an emotionally charged scene, such as a therapy session, within this small, enclosed space serves as a powerful metaphor for the intimacy and complexity of the mind. The interaction between the sculpted forms and the painted interior room creates a multilayered narrative. The contours of the nutshell act as both the physical boundary of the artwork and a representation of psychological boundaries and personal space. There is a sense of vulnerability contrasted with safety, reflecting the complex dynamics often found in therapy itself. The miniature scale encourages an intimate viewing experience, prompting reflection on the delicate nature of emotional recovery and self-exploration.

**Artist Statement - 1998**

I feel that certain objects maintain a poetic sculptural quality. This may be due to the object's grace of form, its aesthetic, or because of its function as metaphoric icon. Using figurative sculpture and painting, my approach to art fuses my personal vision with both traditional ceramic vessel and poetic icon. The situations represented are all based on personal experience, but are usually presented with a twist of the imagination, thus describing my own interpretation and reaction. Humor is used to communicate the absurdities of modern society or as buffer for social statement.

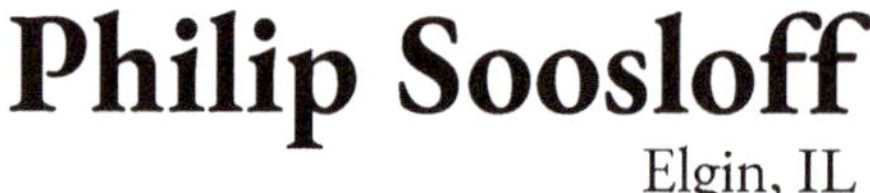

## Philip Soosloff

Elgin, IL

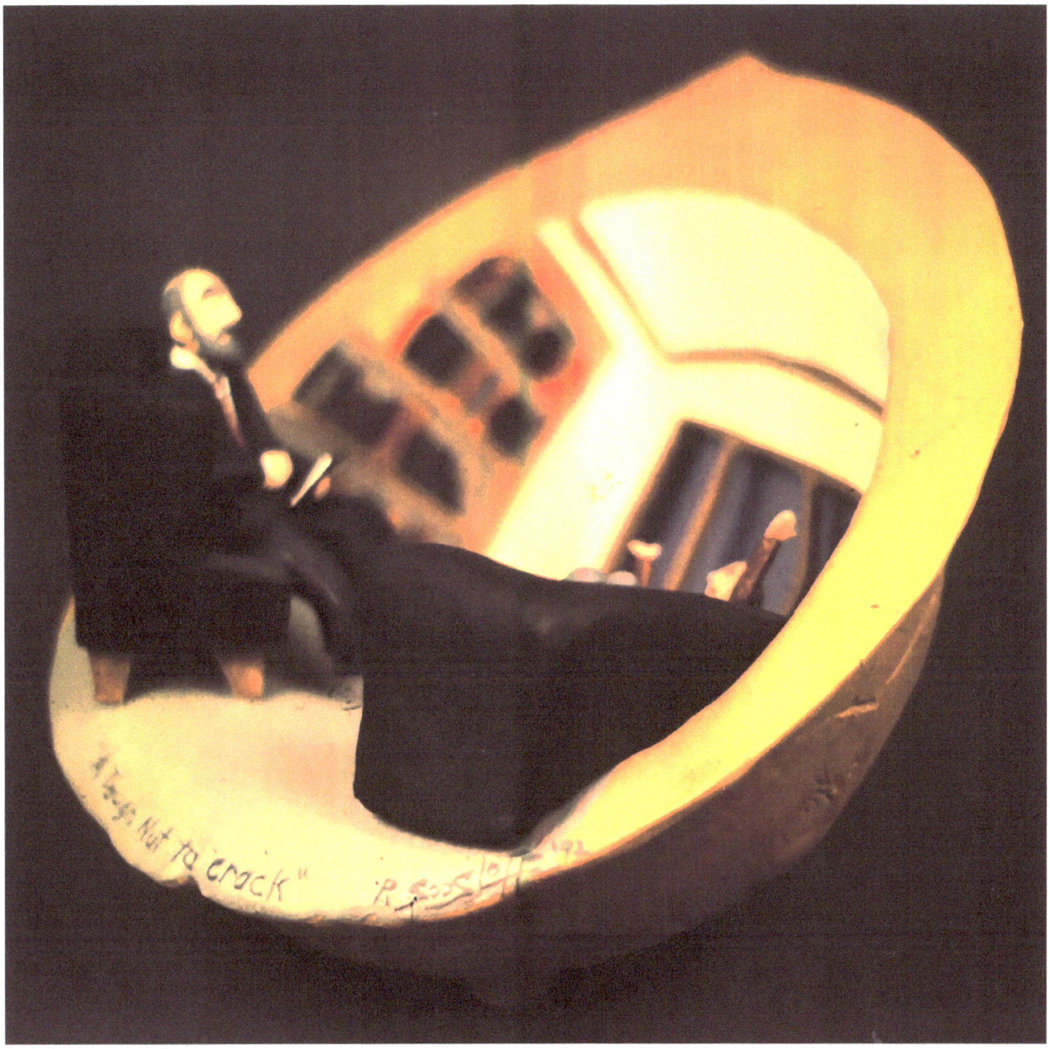

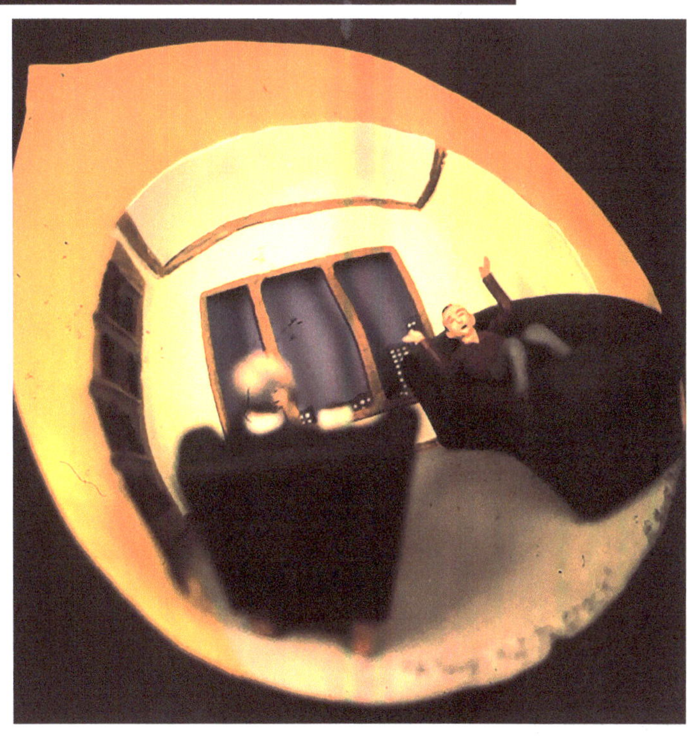

***A Tough Nut to Crack***
clay, metal, paint
9x12x12

# *Secret*

This expressive oil painting portrays a close-up of a person's face with intense focus. The subject has dark, tousled hair with reddish and brown tones, and their gaze is direct and penetrating. The hands are positioned near the face, with fingers curled around the chin and mouth, conveying a sense of contemplation or tension. The use of expressive, almost sculptural brushstrokes brings both vitality and vulnerability to the work. The use of expressive, almost sculptural brushstrokes brings both vitality and vulnerability to the painting. This ability to communicate intense feeling through pose, expression, and surface energy is hypnotic and adds to its emotional accessibility. The direct gaze and hand gesture invite the viewer to explore the interior world of the subject, blurring the line between portraiture and psychological study, supporting the dramatic mood of secrecy.

**Artist Statement - 1998**

To paint the figure is easy, but to paint a figure with emotional meaning is a challenge. I paint my inner world of thoughts, emotions, and perceptions about the external environment. In the painting "Secret" I have used the gesture of hiding the mouth to express the feeling of discomfort when making an utterance or expression.

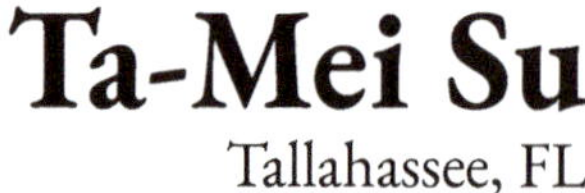


Tallahassee, FL

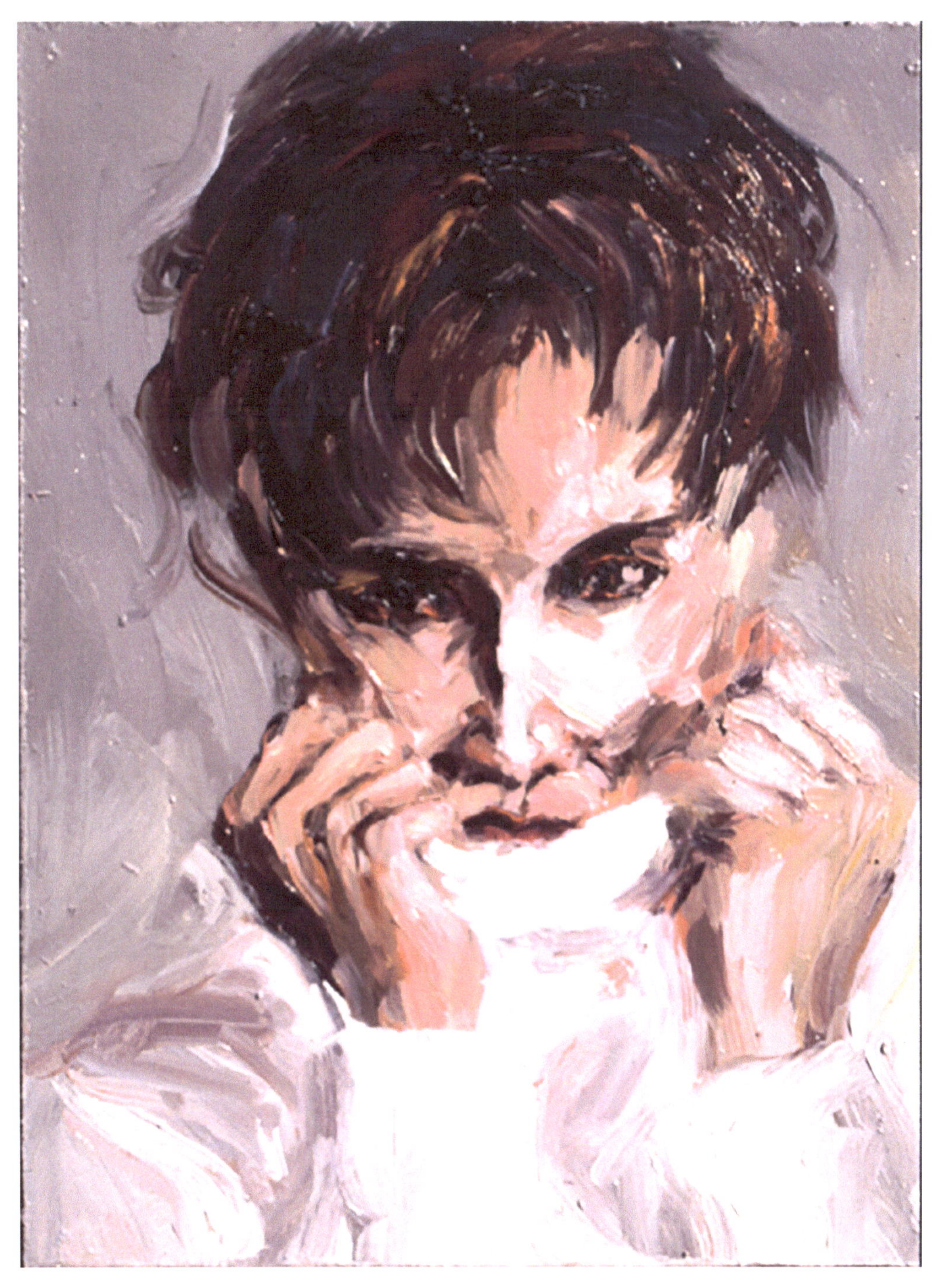

***Secret***
oil on wood
14x11

## *Let's Go*

This acrylic painting focuses on red high-heeled shoes. The vivid red instantly draws the viewer's eye creating a sense of drama and confidence. By isolating just the legs and shoes, an intriguing sense of narrative is acheived allowing the viewer's imagination to fill in the context, which is both playful and open-ended. The swirling background patterns sound especially energetic, and your use of contrasting hues like purples, blues, and whites, punctuated with red and light blue dots, suggests movement and vibrancy. The patterned border, which echoes the interior motifs, frames the composition beautifully. This device helps to contain the energy of the central scene while reinforcing the overall rhythm and unity of the piece. The circular and swirling motifs add a sense of rhythm and continuous motion, imbuing the scene with a musical, almost dance-like quality. The artwork bold color choices, dynamic patterning, and sense of joyful energy has the art feeling both modern and whimsical. This playfulness evokes feelings of joy and excitement, that creates a strong emotional presence.

**Artist Statement - 1998**

I am fascinated by the underlying structures of energy of which all creation is made. I seek to listen to these patterns and express them visually for the world to see.

# Constance Tenhawks

Madison, WI

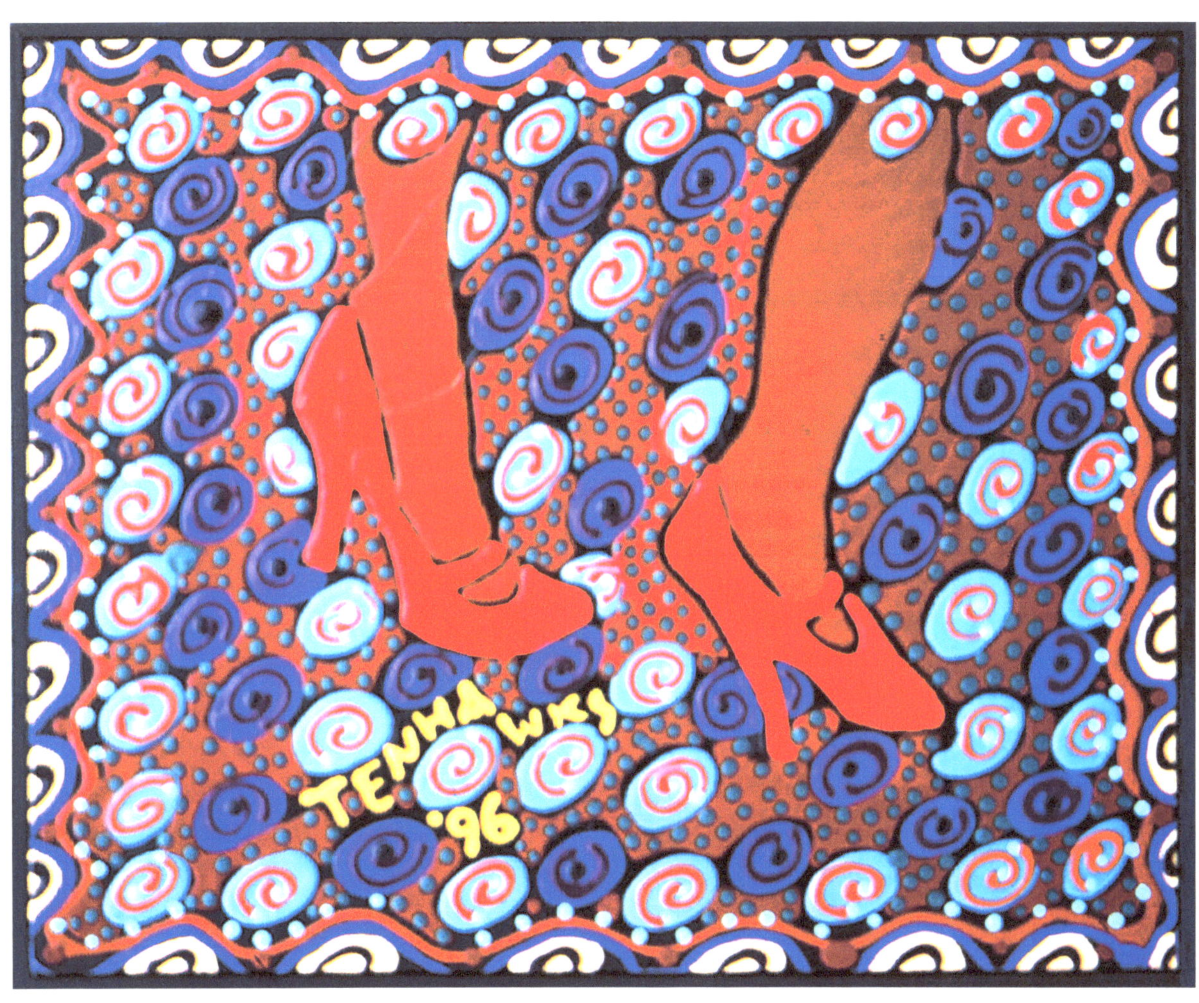


***Let's Go***
Acrylic on canvas
9x12

# Afterwards

The pieces in this book appeared in the national juried exhibition *Current Small Figurative Work in the United States* in 1998 and provide a glimpse into small figurative art in the waning days of this past century. They represent a good sampling of small figurative art in the United States at the end of the twentieth century. These artworks straddle the line of realism, imagination, and abstraction that connects the known and unknown. It demonstrates the peculiar power and expansiveness of small-scale figurative art.

These images show the unique attraction and wide range of small-scale figurative art. The art captures the depths of emotion and life experiences on a personal scale, allowing viewers to approach it. While the tradition of figurative art is ancient, it constantly changes, incorporating abstracted shapes, color, symbolism, and composition to create deep contemplation and feelings in visual stories. It creates an intimacy with its viewer via craftsmanship, detail, and narrative.

With its small size, it opens up new pathways of thinking. The delicacy of the pieces is matched by cultural, philosophical, and emotional depth. Small-scale figurative art is an eternal and persevering medium of human expression with thoughtful and insightful reflection. The pieces capture a unique intimacy between the viewer and the artwork, distilling human experience into compact, yet profoundly expressive moments.

The small scale invites a kind of personal engagement and careful attention that larger works often cannot achieve, creating a space for quiet contemplation and emotional resonance in its practice. It becomes a door to novel ways of thinking. By focusing on craftsmanship and the nuance of detail through subtle gestures or delicate textures, it communicates narrative and emotion within these confined dimensions. It has an engagement with the viewer, providing an intimate environment in which human life is distilled into impactful details.

While the smaller scale presents challenges, finding the balance of techincal precision vs creative exploration, it's also about patience, and being adaptable. But, with those constraints present there are still exciting opportunities to create and even beyond that, bring viewers into an intimate conversation with the images, led by scale as much as content, offering innovation and inviting viewers into an intimate dialogue with the images.

There is indeed a cultural and philosophical weight that the scale brings to bear, influencing both how we think of a work, but also, most importantly, how effectively it speaks to us as human beings. The interplay of tradition and innovation is a conscious effort by the artists to honor the rich history of figurative art while contributing to its evolution in a contemporary context. In today's fast-paced, digitally saturated world, small figurative art is a vital practice. An invitation to slow down and engage with complexity through a tactile, mindful experience.

# Appendix

## Current Small Figurative Work in the United States

**National Juried Exhibition**

Window on Gaines Gallery
Tallahassee, FL 32301
March 27 - April 16, 1998

curated by William Woolf, Ph.D.

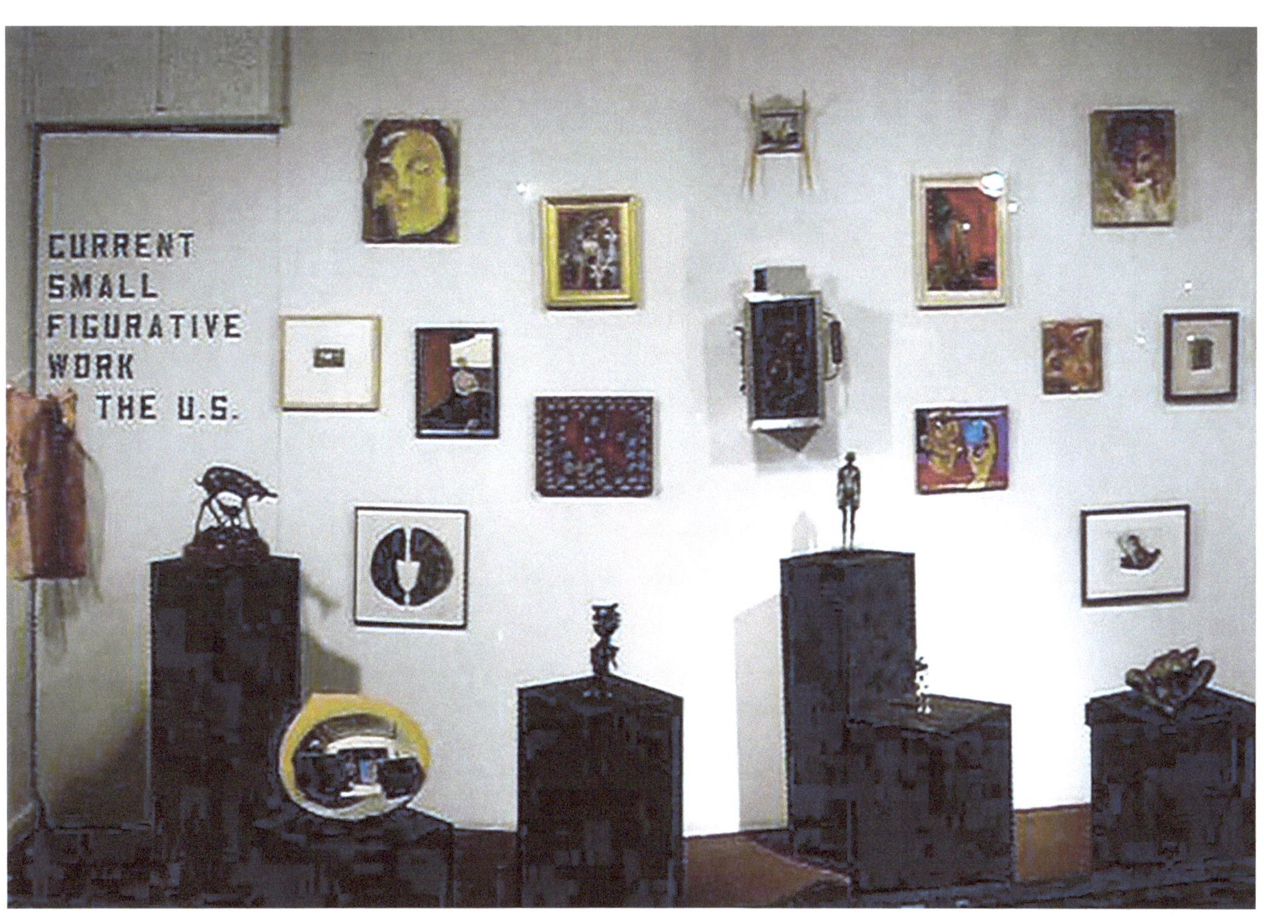

www.ingramcontent.com/pod-product-compliance
Lightning Source LLC
LaVergne TN
LVHW070148110826
845147LV00002B/347
*9781937687229*